GUTS AND GLORY
THE BOMBAY CRICKET STORY

GUTS AND GLORY

THE BOMBAY CRICKET STORY

Sandeep Bamzai

Rupa & Co

Published by
Rupa & Co
7/16, Ansari Road, Daryaganj,
New Delhi 110 002

Offices at:
15 Bankim Chatterjee Street, Kolkata 700 073
135 South Malaka, Allahabad 211 001
PG Solanki Path, Lamington Road, Mumbai 400 007
36, Kutty Street, Nungambakkam, Chennai 600 034
Surya Shree, B-6, New 66, Shankara Park,
    Basavangudi, Bangalore 560 004
3-5-612, Himayat Nagar, Hyderabad 500 029

ISBN 81-7167-611-1

Photo credit: Author and Pradeep Mandhani

Typeset by
Nikita Overseas Pvt Ltd, 1410 Chiranjiv Tower, 43 Nehru Place
New Delhi 110 019

Printed in India by
Rekha Printers Pvt Ltd, A-102/1 Okhla Industrial Area,
Phase-II, New Delhi-110 020

To Anuradha and Aishwarya,
without whose constant support
this wouldn't have been possible

To my parents
who have always encouraged me to write

&

To my sister Kaveree

Contents

Acknowledgements

Hemant Kenkre, a cricketer and friend who pushed me to write my first book and who has been supportive of this venture as well. He took time off to read the manuscript, always on the cellphone asking for the next chapter.

Ajit Wadekar who most graciously allowed me to use photographs from his personal album.

Shirish Shete, once a colleague and now a friend who assisted me by providing several of the pictures in this book.

Sunil Gavaskar, Sachin Tendulkar, Raj Singh Dungarpur, Madhav Mantri, Madhusudan Patil, Ravi Shastri, Bapu Nadkarni, Dilip Vengsarkar, Eknath Solkar, Paddy Shivalkar, Hemant Hadkar, Vasant Raiji, Dilip Sardesai, Vasu Paranjpe, Milind Rege, Naren Tamhane, Sharad Diwadkar, Polly Umrigar, Madhav Apte, Sudhir Naik, G.S. Ramchand, Baloo Gupte, Sanjay Manjrekar, Ajit Wadekar, Ashok Mankad and Sandeep Patil for allowing their minds to be switched on rewind and sharing their memories and thoughts for this book.

Preface

It was in course of writing my first book on cricket two summers ago that it first occurred to me that one needs to look at the genealogy of Bombay's cricket. Though it is politically correct to call the megalopolis Mumbai, in cricketing terms Bombay would be more apt. I can claim to be a Mumbaikar or Bombayite, for I have been living and working in this city of dreams for the last fourteen years. As a resident of this city, I have always found it amazing how almost every era and generation has produced a champion batsman. To understand more about this phenomenon, one needs to look at the sociological import of the game in the city, as also its rapid development. Bombay or Mumbai is a true microcosm of India, a fascinating smorgasbord of faces, hues and religions. An intense megacity, longitudinal, for it is buffeted by the sea on either side, but awesome in size and scope.

A true dream city, for it has a life force which is unique and magnetic, a kinetic energy is all-pervasive and all-encompassing as its people are caught in the hurly-burly of daily life. Despite adversity, calmness is displayed. The same ethos is seen amongst the great batsmen who have walked into the pantheon of fame from Mumbai. Shutting out everything with a singlemindedness of purpose, backed by a commitment to constantly raise the bar. Mumbaikars are resilient folk, not given to buckle under. The harrowing months between December and April in 1992-93 when the city's fabric was torn by communal bloodletting and serial bombing is symptomatic of this resilience and bravado. They have an attitude, described as aloofness or toughness or in the city's singular lingua franca as *kadoosness*. Ravi Shastri, an outsider, a non-Marathi, embodied this spirit in flesh and mind while playing for Don Bosco or Karnataka Sporting Association or Bombay and India. Like many others of his ilk, he ran the gauntlet, waking up at 5.30 a.m taking the suburban train to Azad maidan for practice, finishing up and taking another train back to King's Circle to get to school. Or as Dilip Vengsarkar, who was groomed in the Hindu Colony-Dadar Union school of cricket, says, "Playing to win was what we were taught from an early age and never give your wicket cheap, regardless of which level you were playing at." Undoubtedly a tough lot, for they have to cope with creaking and collapsing amenities. Yet, proud of their heritage and tradition with a will to battle endlessly. Despite the travails that afflict the city-state, many more are attracted to it; trains despatch large new cargoes of humans to its already stretched canvas daily.

The dream city at break point under the baggage of humans carries on producing champions in different walks of life. In all this chaos, cricket has stood the test of time, mirroring its rich mines of talent. Today, there may be talk of Mumbai's cricket floundering, but the fact of the matter is that Sachin Tendulkar continues to play for Bombay. Every time he turns out for Mumbai, the opposition be warned! More importantly, Mumbai, for most part the nation's financial capital, has always been a cricketing powerhouse for ever and ever; breeding not just cricketer after cricketer, but great batsman after batsman. A city-state that has won the Ranji Trophy innumerable times, with fifteen of those titles won in succession.

In my first book, I had dealt with Indian cricket after 1971 and highlighted how the sport had become a metaphor for nationalism. At the vanguard of this change agency were two catalysts according to me—Sunil Gavaskar and Sachin Tendulkar—both batsman with enormous chutzpah, both Bombay bred and both proud Maharashtrians. It was another Bombay batsman, Sanjay Manjrekar, whom I had requested to write the foreword, who actually made me walk the path that I am about to traverse. Manjrekar in many ways is unique, the archetypal middle class Maharashtrian, son of a famous 'son of the soil' Vijay Manjrekar, who learnt the ropes in Shivaji Park, the nursery of both Bombay and Indian cricket. Sanjay Manjrekar made his debut immediately after Gavaskar retired from Test cricket (Gavaskar played his last Test at Bangalore against Pakistan in March, 1987, while Sanjay made his Test debut in the very next Test played by India against the West Indies at Kotla in Delhi in November, 1987, but had to retire hurt when felled by a Winston Benjamin snorter) but represented the same club—Dadar Union. This signalled continuity, for one great Bombay batsman had hung up his boots, only to be replaced by a younger man chasing his own version of the Golden Fleece. Sanjay Manjrekar, along with Sachin Tendulkar and Vinod Kambli made up the troika who were to run with the baton handed over by the likes of Gavaskar, Dilip Vengsarkar and Sandeep Patil.

It was Sanjay Manjrekar who spoke about '*izzat* and *shaurat*', two words now embedded in my lexicon, which young Maharashtrian boys from middle class families thought of when they took to cricket in the Shivaji Park-Hindu Colony area of Dadar. Cricket was a means to get ahead in life. A method to make the tryst with fame and fortune. Cricket, in fact over the last 100 odd years has moved from being a South Mumbai sport to a game which new practitioners took to in this more central part of the city. From a game which first well to do Parsis and then Gujaratis took to like ducks taking to water, it then moved to the Marathi conclave of Shivaji Park-Hindu Colony. On the western side, it is the fabled Shivaji Maharaj's statue which stands over the *maidan* where young boys nurse dreams to play for city and country. This cult of cricket spreads across to the eastern side where educational institutions like R.A. Podar and Ramnarain Ruia college and King George (now rechristened Raja Shivaji Vidyalaya) which overlook the Matunga Maidan stoke the fires. A *maidan* almost as famous as Shivaji Park, for not only Dadar Union play its cricket there, but New Hind too, which produced Pandurang Salgaonkar and Ramakant Achrekar. Shivaji Park Gymkhana on one side and Dadar Union on the other side of the railway tracks battling for Bombay's pride and honour. Azad, Cross and Oval *maidans* were still swarming with young and old cricketers, but the epicentre had shifted to Dadar.

The Parsis, using their stevedoring contacts, were at the vanguard of the cricketing ethos in the city. They wanted to be the mirror image of the ruling British, so what better than to play their game—cricket. The Parsis were instrumental in taking the lead. None greater than one Dr Mehellasha Pavri who as far back as 1878 took 170 wickets on a three month tour of England. As Gerald Howat writing in *Cricket's Second Golden Age* states, "Lord Harris, during his governorship of Bombay in the 1890s, had encouraged the participation of Indians. Under his influence, communal cricket became established in which the different creeds and races within India played each other." Harris cultivated the Parsis, acknowledging the humble, but always loyal and active support of the community. In fact, J.M. Framjee Patel described Harris as the guru of Indian cricket. Before he left Bombay in 1895, the Europeans were playing the Parsis annually and by 1912, they had been joined by the Muslims and Hindus to form the quadrangular, which the Hindus won for the first time in 1919. By 1937, the Rest comprising all the other communities had turned it into a Pentangular.

What Harris had unleashed was a chain reaction—the Parsis wanted to ape the British, the Hindus wanted to do better than the Parsis, followed by the Muslims who wanted to best the other three. A game of one-upmanship and brinkmanship culminated in some of the finest cricket played in the *maidans*. This was largely responsible for Bombay's rich and hoary cricketing heritage. As Gymkhanas sprouted along the art deco Marine Drive in South Mumbai in the form and shape of Hindu, Islam, Parsi and Catholic, so did the magical charm of the game. Cricket flourished and as Richard Cashman wrote so succinctly, "These were events of high symbolic signi-ficance which had been conferred a spiritual blessing of its own." Till finally, the Ranji Trophy came into existence in 1934 when the Maharaja of Patiala presented a golden Grecian urn as a memorial to the legendary Ranjitsinhji who had died the previous year. The game had changed once again. But let the grand old man of Indian cricket Prof D.B. Deodhar, take up the narrative, "Talent which was baulked owing to the narrow and vitiated field of the Quadrangular, found its right avenue and channel in the Ranji Trophy, a championship which Bombay went on to dominate in no uncertain terms."

The Orient Cricket Club was established in 1848 by the Parsis, followed by the creation of the Union Cricket Club in 1866 by the Hindus and the Mohommedan CC in 1883. The Presidency matches which Framjee Patel has described as the Indian derby saw the likes of Col. K.M. Mistry, H.D. Kanga, John Grieg, J.S. Warden, P. Baloo, D.B. Deodhar, Frank Tarrant, C.K. Nayudu, L.P. Jai, Wilfred Rhodes, Syed Wazir Ali, Vijay Merchant, Amar Singh, Syed Mushtaq Ali, Lala Amarnath, Amir Elahi, Vinoo Mankad, Vijay Hazare, Russi Modi *et al* spawn a cricketing cult on the lawns of Bombay Gymkhana. This cult took a tight grip on the city's psyche and sensibilities to make in turn the game of cricket, one of the city's most durable bulwarks.

When Rupa & Co.'s R.K. Mehra very graciously asked to me write this book, I jumped at the opportunity, for it is a subject so close to my heart. I must confess, I played my cricket in Delhi and Calcutta, but Bombay's yearning for combat always fascinated me. As a young cricket writer in Bombay, first at *The Indian Express* and then the *Illustrated Weekly* and *The Sunday Observer*, I just couldn't get enough of the game. For this book, I decided to walk the trail and my recent interaction with several of the legendary names who have turned out in whites for the city-state and nation has only convinced me that Bombay has a unique credo which is mirrored in its cricket. The cricketers themselves from Vasant Raiji who played alongside Vijay Merchant to Sandeep Patil's father Madhusudan Patil to Polly Umrigar to Sunil Gavaskar and Sachin Tendulkar shared their memories with me over endless cups of tea. From Madhav Apte at the CCI to Madhav Mantri in his Hindu Colony home, they were all marvellous raconteurs. This book is my tribute to these soldiers. From Merchant to Manjrekar, from Wadekar to Sardesai, from Gavaskar to Vengsarkar, from Sachin Tendulkar to the next great batsman from the city, the river has flowed ceaselessly; carrying the hopes and aspirations of their countrymen on their shoulders, these soldiers have battled with the best.

And if, as Madhav Apte says with great assertiveness, that cricket is a batsman's game, then Bombay has had a tradition of left arm slow bowlers and leg spinners as well. Palwankar Baloo, Vinoo Mankad who in turn coached Paddy Shivalkar and Eknath Solkar, Subhash Gupte, Bapu Nadkarni have all been connected with Bombay cricket at some stage or the other. As Sunil Gavaskar says, "People forget that the bowlers took wickets and that is how Bombay won its matches. I guess they don't get the recognition due to them." Now increasingly the game is moving out of the congested inner city. The dreams are being burnished in the extended suburbs where the next generation of cricketers are being bred. Gavaskar also reckons that it is the culture of the city that creates tough cricketers and not necessarily the Maharashtrian psyche which he feels is overdone. He believes that Ravi Shastri exemplified this spirit best, for he played the game harder than anybody else, as he sallied forth, trained in the rudiments of survival by a megacity. Yet, the necessity of role models cannot be underplayed, as one generation of cricketers followed another, son followed father, nephew followed uncle and so the cycle continues. The I (inspirational) factor is what I call it. Vasu Paranjpe adds that the proximity to *maidans* is the single biggest reason for so many cricketers to come through. Agreed, but for so many of those cricketers to make the cut in the harsh and often brutal world of international cricket is what I am specifically trying to focus on.

This emanates from a culture of discipline and being ruthlessly competitive. Or to take another word out of Bombay's language—playing with a *khunnas*. Here I would like to recount a story. In a Rajasthan versus Bombay Ranji match, one of the innumerable times the two sides were involved, Dilip Sardesai was 'Mankaded' by Kailash Gattani. Sardesai was furious, for the bowler did not give him a warning prior to knocking down the stumps in his follow through, even as Sardesai was backing up as the non-striker. As Sardesai says, "Gattani could have never got me out. I guess this was the only way he could have dismissed me." Anyway, Sardesai was hopping mad, so when the Bombay captain Ajit Wadekar at 450 odd for 5 was planning to declare, Sardesai locked up Wadekar in the bathroom and Bombay carried on batting, scoring over 600 runs. Poetic justice or reprisal, this was Sardesai or 'Sardee man's' answer to Gattani's mode of dismissing him.

Today, the same ethos is beginning to be reflected in Karnataka and in Hyderabad where the flame of Gundappa Vishwanath, Brijesh Patel and Mohammed Azharuddin and M.L. Jaisimha is being kept alive by the likes of Rahul Dravid and V.V.S. Laxman. The game has spread to every nook and cranny in India as it abounds in not just players but savants. But despite the paradigm shift, Bombay remains India just as India remains Bombay, a true mirror image, a cosmopolitan gargantuan which has produced an assembly line of cricketers. A set of players which has never given quarter, nor asked for one in any joust. Determined and driven, their mindsets have never entertained failure. Boys whose first dalliance with the game was with tennis ball cricket in the lanes and *gullies* that stamp the topography of the city grew up to be men who carried the burden of a nation. A rag tag army of individuals looked upto these icons for deliverance. This is the story of Bombay cricket, its icons, its work ethic and its cultural and sociological background...

1 | Boys from Chikalwadi

BOMBAY CRICKET'S EDIFICE, BUILT BY THE PARSIS AND honed on Presidency cricket, is multi-layered. A strong foundation has naturally meant a widespread fervour for the game. It is the layers, however, that propelled the game forward at all times—schools, collegiate, club and office cricket—all enablers which meant that not quality players, but a quantity of quality players came through with unerring regularity. Unceasing waves would be an apt description of this amazing talent pool. Cricketers from the sixties will tell you of Bharat Narvekar who was one of the best seam bowlers of his time, but all he managed was a solitary Irani Trophy game. The State Banker never got to play Ranji Trophy.

If the A division of the Kanga League had formidable outfits like Dadar Union, Shivaji Park Gymkhana, Sunder CC, Baronet, Parsi Cyclists, Matunga Gymkhana, National,

New Hind, United, CCI, Hindu Gymkhana and Khar Gymkhana, then the Times of India Shield saw the Tatas, ACC, Kohinoor Mills, Cipla, Western Railway, SBI, Mafatlals (the true powerhouse, winning the title eight times in a row) and Nirlon battle for supremacy. It was all about raising the bar, performing consistently and constantly at every level to make it to the next level. The grind was remorseless and the pressure relentless, but the boys braved the competitive edge to become men. Men turned into icons with their stirring deeds and bravado. Sounds like hyperbole. No, there are record books to prove the style and substance that is associated with Bombay's cricket. Adrenalised and energised as these young men were by a cult of cricket that was almost magical and devotional. Living in cocoons, isolationists who lived, ate and breathed the game. Bombay cricketers had a character, an inner strength that goaded them into a continuous pursuit of excellence. Thirty-four Ranji Trophy titles, including fifteen on the trot and fifteen Irani Trophy wins. Above all, they had a passion and an unsatiated thirst for the game. In all this, there were some that were first among equals.

In Chikalwadi, near Bhatia Hospital, Bhagirathi building is where in typical middle class surroundings, two small boys dreamt the dream that has made many a Bombayite traverse the path to fame and fortune. Sunil Gavaskar and Milind Rege were best friends from an early age, collecting pictures of cricketers from *Sport & Pastime* magazine and pasting them in ledgers which Sunil's father Manohar Gavaskar would bring from the office. These two boys obsessed with cricket read voraciously on cricket and played mock games in the lane below with a portion of the garage door functioning as the wicket. Joined by other kids like Sudhir Naik and Sharad Hazare (who went on to play for Bombay), among others, the boys of Chikalwadi lived in a dream world. Cricket was omnipresent, for Sunil's father Manohar used to play the game. More importantly, Sunil's uncle was Madhav Mantri (who has been living in his Hindu Colony house since 1939), a Dadar Union and Bombay stalwart. But Sunil who loved imitating Ray Lindwall and bowling fast as a child was fascinated by another sport as well. As Sunil says, "My uncle Shashikant Gavaskar was a wrestling buff and he would take us to Vallabhbhai Patel stadium for the *dangals* (a precursor to the more popular World Wrestling Federation) featuring Dara Singh. Milind would also come occasionally. Yes, cricket was ubiquitous, for it was everywhere around us. The gang would play downstairs with tennis ball in the *gully*, just as thousands played it all around the city." Gavaskar also remembers visiting the *maidans*, in the main to watch Fort Vijay CC play. As one grew up, Gavaskar says, "Those days time spent on Azad maidan was time well spent. For there was a unique thrill and inspiration associated with being on the same *maidan* as some of the legends and sharing *khara* biscuits and *chai* in the same tent as Ramakant Desai, Farokh Engineer or Bapu Nadkarni. It was like being in the presence of the extraordinary."

There are tales about Gavaskar's fabled powers of concentration and how he hated getting out, even at an early age. If declared leg before the wicket and unhappy with the decision, young Sunil would walk away with the bat and the game would abruptly get over. His counter to that affirmative action even today is, "Come on, I knew where my off stump was even then." Sunil Gavaskar is not being presumptuous, he is merely speaking his mind about a credo of confidence which comes from being near perfect at a particular task. Enough has been written about Gavaskar and his middle class background, but one needs to piece together some of the parts of the jigsaw that made him the world's leading run scorer (till Allan Border overtook him) and the highest scorer of centuries. In a city which had given Indian cricket Vijay Merchant and Vijay Manjrekar, it was only logical and a matter of time for the next great batsman to come through.

Gavaskar remembers the sheer competitiveness of Bombay's cricket when he began to wind his way up the ranks. His compatriot and friend Milind Rege, a fine player himself, but debilitated by a heart problem at a young age, followed his career with great interest, even as he played alongside Gavaskar. In a Cooch Behar game against East Zone, Khandu Rangnekar told then presiding deity amongst batsmen Vijay Manjrekar to have a look at Sunil Gavaskar. His words were simple and telling, "Come and watch a young man play!" Manjrekar was impressed, for the young man notched up a double hundred. So were others when the young man known as G. Sunil began to make waves and his ascent in Bombay's cricket. In November, 1963, the same G. Sunil had earned his first mention in despatches in the *Free Press Journal*, scoring an unbeaten 30, batting at number 10 (Rege had batted number nine) in a Harris Shield match on Azad maidan for his school St Xavier's. But the G. Sunil of 1963 vintage was to earn accolades from the fourth estate and this time rightly by his proper name Sunil Gavaskar.

By January 1965, Milind Rege recounts how the duo joined hands to put together a 310 run partnership for the second wicket against Maratha High School led by one Eknath Solkar in the Harris Shield. Gavaskar will tell you that Xavier's, though a Jesuit school with no real cricketing background became a hotbed for the sport when it reached the final in 1959-60 (those days played to the finish) at the Brabourne Stadium. As the stadium had been booked for only four days and the match didn't show any signs of getting over, the game was shifted to a new venue—Cross maidan. Sunil wasn't old enough to play in that final, but the entire school was galvanized by that victory notched up by Xavier's. Practice balls at Xavier's used to be polished with Cherry Blossom shoe polish and what passed off as a pitch was half a mat on a long rectangle of mud which was partly stone at the Liberty cricket ground opposite Bombay Hospital. This was where Milind Rege, Sunil Gavaskar and Atul Mankad, contemporaries, practised their cricket. Rege remembers those days fondly saying that one would get a reward of Rs. 1.25 for lunch if the team reached the semi-finals and a coke and movie was the carrot after the final.

These boys and many like them aspired to break into the big league. Interestingly, Manohar Gavaskar was an attractive player, who turned out for Rajasthan and Forbes Campbell. Sunil's uncle Madhav Mantri recalls how Vinoo

Mankad would call out to him, "George (Mantri was known as George for his resemblance to George Headley), *aisa player mangta hai, shotmaker hona chaiya* (referring to Manohar Gavaskar)." In many ways, Sunil followed both his father and uncle, but his obsession and desire to be first among equals took him to the zenith. The famous story about Sunil visiting his uncle's (Mantri) home in Hindu colony bears repetition here. As a small boy, Sunil came to Mantri's house, when the 'nana mama' was getting ready for a Sunday game. Seeing the cupboard full of caps, Sunil asked his mama for one. But Mantri, always a disciplinarian, admonished the boy saying that the cap had to be earned and not asked for. Gavaskar was troubled by the incident and a couple of years later earned his first cap and sweater from Nana mama when as an opening bowler for Xavier's, he did well in a Giles Shield match. Nana mama, always a major influence on the young boy then told him this was merely the beginning.

Madhav Mantri says, "Once I returned from office and a slightly disconsolate Sunil told me that the close of play score is 400 for one and I have got out for 200. This is when I mentioned to him, never throw your wicket away." Always learning and imbibing skills, Sunil scored a triple century in a Purshottam Shield final for Dadar Union. After scoring his 300th run, he took fresh guard and left the next ball bowled to him in the channel of uncertainty, without flirting with it. Vasu Paranjpe, one of the leading lights of Dadar Union and now a prominent coach, turned to Mantri and asked him, "Skipper, why is he doing that?" And Mantri's reply was, "because he is learning". Incidentally when Sunil returned to the tent, he was asked why he didn't attack recklessly after scoring 300, his counter came pat, "Why should I throw my wicket away?"

Mantri believes that determination, dedication, discipline and desire were the cornerstones of Sunil Gavaskar's cricketing career. For instance, as he was preparing for international cricket, he promised his mother that he would never touch liquor and stuck to that promise for the rest of his career. A very good observer who showed immense talent as a mimic as well, cloned Mantri's square cut at a young age. Mantri remembers that Sunil and Milind would come to watch ACC in the Times Shield games. Memorable incidents are aplenty about Gavaskar's methodical rise. But the inexorable influence that his Madhav mama had on him is a tale by itself. When Sunil was selected in the reserves for the Duleep Trophy, the dates overlapped with the inter-university (Rohinton Baria) in Pune where he was appointed Bombay's captain. The young man was in a dilemma. Mantri decided the course of action. Sunil went to Pune and smashed 774 runs in three matches including an innings of 327. Vijay Merchant, then chairman of the national selection committee stated, "Here is a run hungry player."

Milind Rege, sitting in his Tata Steel office in Bombay House, slapbang in the middle of Mumbai's business district, will tell you that the difference between Sunil and him was clearly ambition. Mirroring what Mantri describes as desire, Rege says, "I played four years before him, he was always India class, I wasn't. As children when we had gone to Madhav mama's house and Sunil had been roundly told off after wearing the cap, Sunil nursed a burning desire to get to the top. Blessed as he was with innate powers of concentration and patience, it was only a matter of time." Rege, like Sunil, feels that the importance of inter-schools and inter-collegiate cricket has eroded rapidly over the years. Bombay University and St Xavier's kept producing players with unerring regularity. Rege remembers how Xavier's alone produced eight Ranji players—Ashok Mankad, Kailash Gattani (who played for Rajasthan), Ramesh Nagdev, Sunil, Mahesh Sampat, Atul Mankad and himself. These stepping-stones have lost their importance and the last two stars who came out of these mills were the firm of Sachin Tendulkar and Vinod Kambli who played for Shardashram in the Harris Shield. Rege himself, according to Paranjpe had an exquisite back-foot off-drive and was a good player of the quicker bowlers. In 1965-66, Eknath Solkar captained the Indian schoolboys' side against their London counterparts. Other members of the side—Ramesh Nagdev, Sunil Gavaskar, Milind Rege and Ajit Naik. When Indian schoolboys visited Ceylon in 1963-64, Kailash Gattani was captain and the side included Ramnath Parkar, Eknath Solkar, Kiran Ashar and Ramesh Nagdev.

Of course, role models have always played a part in Bombay's cricket. Rege thought of Manohar Hardikar when he batted, Sunil in turn copied M.L. Jaisimha's walk, while Dilip Vengsarkar and Sanjay Manjrekar modelled themselves on Sunil. Pertinently, Mantri was so sincere that he never selected Sunil for Dadar Union initially. By then Sunil had moved to Hindu Colony, so he began playing in the B division for Rajasthan. By the time he moved to Dadar

Union, cricket was highly competitive. For instance Dadar Union had Vasu Paranjpe, Sunil Gavaskar, Ramnath Parkar, Dilip Vengsarkar (in the seventies) and Milind Rege. To provide a flavour of what the other teams were like, Shivaji Park Gymkhana had Ajit Wadekar, Sudhakar Adhikari, Paddy Shivalkar, Ajit Pai, Ajit Naik, Baloo Gupte, Abdul Ismail while Hindu Gymkhana had Budhi Kunderan, Dilip Sardesai, Sharad Diwadkar, Eknath Solkar, Bapu Nadkarni, Umesh Kulkarni and Sharad Hazare in their ranks and Parsi Cyclists were represented by Russi Surti, Meli and Behram Irani, Farokh Engineer, Noshir Tantra and Nari Contractor. While the battle of the roses on the lines of the famous Yorkshire versus Lancashire existed between Dadar Union and Shivaji Park Gymkhana, there was also a battle between South Mumbai's two hot teams—Hindu Gymkhana and Parsi Cyclists. Moreover, these four teams were always at each other's throats in the sixties and seventies.

Cricket was flourishing in the city, just as it had done earlier. Almost round the year cricket was being played—Kanga League, Police Shield, Comrades Shield, Purshottam Shield, Times Shield, Padmakar Talim Shield (which incidentally is the world's first 50 over one day tournament, started in 1948) and of course the Ranji, Duleep and Irani Trophies. Outside Bombay too, there was the Buchi Babu and the Moin-ud-Dowla tournaments in which Bombay cricketers were regulars. On his first class debut in the Irani Trophy, Gavaskar failed in both innings (0 & 4), but after a spell in the wilderness, he came roaring back with 176 against Rajasthan in the Ranji Trophy. Dropped off the first ball by Sugaveer Singh off Kailash Gattani's bowling, he took full toll. This was also the time that Ajit Wadekar was unstoppable and as Rege says, "All those who played under him had the highest regard for him as captain and batsman." Rege who had a distinguished Ranji career, taking 106 wickets with his off spin and scoring 1124 runs in 41 matches claims that a Bombay player had to constantly perform those days, for the bench strength was inordinately strong. Failure meant an exit. Such was the commitment and peer pressure that nobody wanted to miss a game. A story about Sudhakar Adhikari is often told. Adhikari got married in the morning, turned up to play a Ranji game and attended his own reception the same evening. Similarly, Rege did not attend his childhood friend Sunil's nuptials either, for he was playing a Ranji game in Junagadh.

As Gavaskar began to settle down in the Ranji side, his opening partner Ramesh Nagdev was rapidly making a name for himself. Rege says Nagdev was more attacking, correct and courageous at that point of time. Nari Contractor thought highly of him and hence took him to Gujarat. In his first Ranji game against Bombay, he hooked Umesh Kulkarni for six off the first ball. But the lure of lucre took him to California. The highest score ever recorded in a Harris Shield game is still credited to Nagdev who smashed an unbeaten 427 for Hindi Vidyabhavan in 1963-64 against Amin H.S. In the 1965-66 season, Nagdev scored another triple century, this time 304 against Hume H.S. Incidentally, the aforementioned Umesh Kulkarni toured Australia in 1967-68, played a handful of Tests and on his return never found a regular place in the Bombay side. Sunil Gavaskar, meanwhile was the marathon man, like vintage wine getting better all the time. One of his better known knocks during his formative years was a 25 and 10 on a fresh pitch at the CCI. Turning out for the Combined Universities against a New Zealand attack in 1969, boasting of Dayle Hadlee and Dick Collinge, Gavaskar showed glimpses of his exemplary technique. Back in 1965-66, Gavaskar had scored four successive hundreds in the Harris Shield, but could not emulate Vijay Merchant who batting for Bharda had scored a 100 in each innings as far back as 1926. Kiran Ashar who later played for Bombay was another prolific Harris Shield batsman. In 1963-64, he hit two hundreds in a match against Balmohan Vidyamandir, and twice, first in the same season and later in 1964-65, scored five successive hundreds. A record that still stands. And Ashar did not play for India.

Just how did Gavaskar, the boy who used to imitate Ray Lindwall and Wes Hall as a child become an opener? Rege as captain of St Xavier's asked Sunil to open against Anjuman-e-Islam. Sunil who by then was batting at number three wasn't particularly happy, but since the captain had ordered went ahead and took the plunge into the deep end. In an inter-collegiate final, the Rege-Gavaskar combine who played so much of their cricket together added 430 runs against Siddarth College. Gavaskar was on his way ... Gavaskar himself says, "I was fighting for a place and when I was out of the Bombay side, I played a lot of inter-university cricket. Just prior to the tour of the West Indies when I finally got a look in, I scored zero and was almost out for the same score in the second innings as well. But Saeed Ahmed Hattea was bowling quick and I took a couple of catches." However, in the final against Rajasthan, he got that big hundred mentioned earlier. This was also the time that Vijay Merchant, an inspirational figure in Bombay cricket took a liking to Gavaskar. As Gavaskar says, Merchant was most encouraging, taking time to talk to him. He says, "Vijay Manjrekar would also come regularly to the CCI and talk to us." The penchant for big scores came from the discipline instilled at Dadar Union and Bombay. Gavaskar doesn't think it is such a big deal, "It is not a special talent, I sincerely feel that every batsman worth his salt should realise that he needs to maximise whenever he is on a roll." Before he went to the West Indies, Gavaskar's fledgling first class career which was working in fits and starts was nothing much to write about. He had played 12 first class games, stretching back to 1966-67, making 811 runs.

Vasu Paranjpe is another important component in the Sunil Gavaskar jigsaw. Tales of Gavaskar's commitment are told even today. That he would return from England in the dead of the night and ring up Paranjpe at six a.m. saying that he should be played in the Dadar Union side that same day. This high level of efficiency is something that Sunny Gavaskar dismisses now, saying that it was the done thing, for the club's honour was foremost. In fact, Paranjpe revealed that Sunny even today has given standing instructions that if Dadar Union is a player short then he will pad up. Paranjpe reckons that Gavaskar played his cricket like a chief accountant while Gundappa Vishwanath played his version expansively like a sales manager spending money on office account. The other notable difference between the two great Indian contemporaries and now brothers-in-law, according to Paranjpe was that Sunil played the ball and the bowler, while Vishy played the ball. For Sunil cricket was as much a mind game, even while it was a physical activity.

The boy who made his mother bowl to him as a child batted for 13132 minutes in Test cricket for 10122 runs, scoring 81 first class hundreds. Interestingly, 39 per cent of Sunny's total first class runs came in Test cricket. What made this man so special, after all others too grew up in the same middle class neighbourhoods all over the city? Desire and ambition, the seeds of which he has sown. The torch has been carried by Dilip Vengsarkar and now Sachin Tendulkar. Sunny himself will tell you that cricket those days was a vehicle for employment opportunity. Since the Times Shield was so important, offices employed good cricketers. Vitally, cricket provided security for life to these cricketers. Yes, he agrees, that what one made out of the job depended on the person concerned. For instance, Nirlon that had a team in the lower division used Sunny as a catalyst. By bringing in a Test player like Sunny, Virenechee Sagar built the team around him and declared his intent of winning the Times Shield. Sunny in turn recruited Karsan Ghavri, Sandeep Patil, Suresh Shastri, Rakesh Tandon and Suru Nayak among others and yet could never win the Times Shield. Such was the level of competition.

Sudhir Naik was one of the boys from Chikalwadi, though he used to stay further up at Forjet Hill. He would come and play tennis ball cricket in the *gullies*. He says, "I think the sense of balance, technique and purpose that came from playing those tennis ball matches made us sounder players. All of us—Milind Rege, Sunil Gavaskar, Kishore Rao, Sudhakar Shetty, Sharad Hazare and myself— played this form of underarm tennis ball cricket. The key was to play straight and keep the ball on the ground all the time." I guess this brand of tennis ball cricket must have resulted in better players being produced, for most of them went to have distinguished careers. Sudhir's brother Anil also played in those matches, while his cousin Ajit Naik went on to play for all-India schools and Bombay. The nucleus of the Bombay side of the late 1960s and early 1970s actually grew up together and played alongside one another from an early age, both at school, college, domestic and international levels. As Sudhir Naik says, "The Bombay University side had some real heavyweights—Sunil Gavaskar, Kailash Gattani, Sudhir Naik, Ashok Mankad, Mahesh Sampat and Ramesh Nagdev." Gavaskar, Mankad and Solkar became comrades in arms on the twin tours of West Indies and England.

In 1983, Sunil Gavaskar had a lean time, first in the West Indies where he struggled for runs—20, 0, 1, 32, 147 not out, 2, 19, 18 & 1—against Malcolm Marshall, Andy Roberts, Joel Garner and Michael Holding and then in the World Cup. Rumourmongers had a field day—Gavaskar was unhappy under Kapil Dev's captaincy. But the loss of form had begun much earlier on the tour of Pakistan where Imran Khan's vicious indipper had laid many a reputation low. Gavaskar with the added burden of captaincy was really under the cosh and only Mohinder Amarnath came through unscathed as the Indian side's psyche was completely brutalised. In Pakistan, Gavaskar had scored 83, 8, 42, 12, 127 not out, 17, 60, 13, 5 and 67. Imran Khan scalped him five times, but more significantly, the series saw the end of G.R. Vishwanath's playing career. A crisis of confidence gripped Gavaskar, further accentuated in the opening Test against the West Indies at Kanpur later that same year. Marshall dismissed him in both innings, the bat being wrenched out of Gavaskar's hands due to the pace and lift of the delivery. It was a shocker that most Gavaskar junkies could not come to terms with. And that too in his *maika*. Gavaskar was disconsolate, he even contemplated chucking it up. Against this backdrop, he went to mentor Vasu Paranjpe. Paranjpe says, "He came home and we discussed what had transpired at Kanpur. I told him there are four fast bowlers in the opposition and you cannot defend. The best thing would be to attack. I gave him the example of Stan McCabe in the bodyline series when he launched a counter-attack against Larwood and Voce." The next game was at the Kotla in Delhi. Sitting in the dressing room, Gavaskar, who always was in a world of his own while preparing for the game told Prabhu Desai, the then BCA secretary in a rare display of emotion, "*Aaj baag*, I will show them. The bat fell out of my hands, I will show them today." Telling words those, which once again provide an insight into how Gavaskar's mind functioned. Pride and passion were intertwined in the man's karma. He wanted to be the master of his own destiny.

Gavaskar slammed a 100 in 94 balls, his first 50 coming

off just 37 balls. There was intent and defiance. Moreover, his pride had been dented. Sunil Gavaskar was back in business. Similarly in the next Test at Ahmedabad, the West Indies after being bowled out for 281, saw Gavaskar launch another assault, 40 out of the first 50 came in only nine overs, finally succumbing to Holding for 90. Once again the crowds rallied around their hero. At Bombay in the next Test, even though India was taking a beating, the *hoi polloi* gathered to see Gavaskar go past Bradman's record of 29 centuries. But Sunil failed, scoring 12 and 3. And then came Calcutta and its Eden where the crowds congregated to see Gavaskar flay the West Indians (this writer was one of thousands who flocked the stadium that day). Before one could say Sunil Gavaskar, he was out to the very first ball of the match to his nemesis Malcolm Marshall. The second essay raised expectations once again as Gavaskar started in his usual (for that particular series) style, eschewing caution and playing his shots. In a matter of moments it was all over, Gavaskar played an expansive square cut of Holding and was caught for 20. The crowds jeered and derisive comments were made about Gavaskar for which he did not forgive the Calcuttans for a long time, even missing a Test match later in his career.

Once again a crisis of confidence loomed large as Gavaskar battled with his inner self, pained by comments about his not trying enough. The Gavaskar-Kapil Dev battle was also at its height. Once again Gavaskar thought of calling it a day. Once again his mentors Mantri and Paranjpe counseled him—the former told him to fake an injury while Paranjpe was upset with the way he had batted in Calcutta. And in almost cinematic style, while shaving in the morning, Sunil Gavaskar decided against quitting and playing at Madras. Sounds dramatic! But Gavaskar was always the proud Maharashtrian, a gunslinger who would aim for the heart when slighted. At Madras, the West Indians batted first scoring 313, Gavaskar decided to drop down the order, a decision taken during the famous rapprochement in Delhi between him and Kapil where board president N.K.P. Salve had played peacemaker. Well, what do you know, India was 0 for 2 with both Anshuman Gaekwad and Vengsarkar consumed by India's *bete noire* Marshall. A familiar looking Gavaskar dropped anchor. Slowly the tide turned as he ground his way to 236 not out.

Earlier in 1981, a problem with his technique had resulted in a similar loss of form. A lean patch in Australia and New Zealand where Dennis Lillee and Richard Hadlee proved to be his bugbears. Unsure of where his off stump was, Gavaskar was struggling. His scores 0, 10, 23, 5, 10, 70, 23, 12, 53, 5 & 33. Apparently, the late Russi Modi used to write regularly to Bradman who used to reply. Modi asked Bradman who was always a keen watcher of cricket, why Sunil was struggling—was it a fault in technique. Bradman's answer was interesting: There is nothing wrong with Sunny's technique, he has put on weight and as such his reflexes are just that wee bit slower for our wickets and our bowlers. Gavaskar analysed this on his return, he even asked both Polly Umrigar and Madhav Mantri to watch him bat. Gavaskar says, "Instead of the part step back and across that I was taking, I was shuffling, with the result, I wasn't very sure where my off stump was." As a result of this, Gavaskar was eventually moving towards the off stump from his original guard. The video came to his rescue, as did tips from some of the older players.

Players from Bombay have developed well from being positioned slapbang in the middle of a cricketing microcosm. Men like Gavaskar, Rege and Naik played with distinction at different levels. Bradman had high regard for Gavaskar. When somebody asked him as to who was superior between Geoff Boycott and the Indian master, Sir Don said that obviously Sunny for he had better shot making ability, while Boycott was completely a grafter and overly defensive. That is why it is surprising that Bradman chose Arthur Morris and Barry Richards over Gavaskar. Another time, Gavaskar writing to Paranjpe from Australia said that Bradman had come looking for him so that he could take him for lunch at the Adelaide Oval. Gavaskar was sitting and watching Jeff Thomson bowl, wearing a kurta and jeans, when Bradman abruptly showed up. Sir Don sat with Gavaskar and told him that in his present attire, he would not be allowed to go into the committee room. Though lunch was not on the menu, Bradman spoke to Sunny and told him that while the tall men have power, small men like them have the footwork.

When Gavaskar did finally announce his retirement, Paranjpe tried hard to change his mind, for he argued that Gavaskar should play the winter series against the West Indies and complete a cricketing cycle, but as Sunny himself says, "I wasn't enjoying the game any more. Particularly while fielding. I had begun to look at the clock—waiting for lunch or tea or close of play to come along. If you aren't enjoying the game, it is best to get out!"

Sudhir Naik actually ended up opening with his former chum Gavaskar, but unfortunately only once at Edgbaston in 1974. His Test appearances were limited to three (141 runs with 77 as his highest), but he did lead Bombay to the Ranji trophy in 1971, when the crème de la crème of Bombay's batting was touring. Naik was a sound cricketer who used the breeding ground of college and *maidan* cricket to vault to the top. Playing for National CC, a club that he coaches now, Naik remembers the battles with the top players of that era—Polly Umrigar, Hanumant Singh, Vasant Amladi, Ramakant Desai, Ghulam Guard, Farokh Engineer, Behram and Meli Irani. He says that this exposure against top class cricketers at a very young age toughened him. Not only did these matches prepare and ready him for sterner Tests; the Times Shield matches which saw 'outsiders' like Uday Joshi, Brijesh Patel, Tiger Pataudi, Karsan Ghavri and Dhiraj Parsanna sharpened his skills. Vinoo Mankad was coaching in Bombay during Naik's formative years. At the L.R. Tairsee nets on the Hindu Gymkhana lawns, the almost larger than life Mankad would give Bombay's best young cricketers tips. Naik, Ashok Mankad, Sharad Hazare, Sunil Purohit *et al* were trained by Mankad. Of the wards, Naik was the only one who hadn't played school cricket. Naik remembers that he used to bowl fastish leg breaks in those nets and Mankad was a strict disciplinarian. The nets would begin at 6.30 a.m and if anyone was late Vinoobhai would make him do 10 rounds. When Pakistan visited India in 1960-61, Polly Umrigar seeking practice against leg spin (since Pakistan had Inthikab Alam in their ranks) came to the Tairsee nets where young Naik bowled to him. Leg breaks were consigned to the rubbish heap, as Naik too turned into an opener for his college, first Ruparel and then Siddarth.

Such was the aura of the game, leading to interaction between the young and the old that cricket was always the winner. The young were always being educated on cricket's learning curve by masters who seemed to be there to impart their skills to the next generation. This cycle has been most beneficial for the game in the city.

2 | Shishyas who became Gurus

IF SUNIL GAVASKAR RETIRED FROM CRICKET IN 1987, THE next flagbearer of the Bombay batting bastion was already playing alongside him and scoring handsomely. His name was Dilip Balwant Vengsarkar. Radically different from Gavaskar and other Bombay batsman of the past, he was tall and upright. While he was associated with Gavaskar in several notable partnerships for Dadar Union, Bombay and India, he really came into his own after Sunil retired. Vengsarkar, a wicket-keeper batsman initially, exploded on the cricket firmament with nothing short of a big bang. Trained in the art of warfare and cricket at the very best breeding ground, Vengsarkar, another son of the soil, was a logical successor to Gavaskar's throne.

But let Vengsarkar himself take up the narrative, "There was only one game played in Hindu Colony and the same game was actively encouraged at King George where I studied. There were Test players in every lane, cricket was pouring out of ever nook and cranny." Vengsarkar joined Dadar Union immediately after school, a team that had luminaries like Vasu Paranjpe, V.S. (Marshall) Patil, Sunil Gavaskar and Ramnath Parkar. For good measure, Shivaji Park Gymkhana wasn't far enough. Cricket was top of mind. Club cricket had tremendous significance attached to it and with international engagements few and far between, cricketers played for pride and to win. Vengsarkar will tell you that Dadar Union was the best place to make one's debut. Vengsarkar remembers how DU won the Kanga league for five years in a row, immediately after he joined the club in 1973. The key according to him was that DU showed discipline in their cricket and always displayed an attacking mien.

Vengsarkar feels that those days were completely different, for when he started out, he never thought of even making the Bombay team. A different ethos and paradigm existed where young cricketers like him were in awe of the heavyweights in the side, watching and learning while playing with them. This attitude honed on the *maidan* stood the young man in good stead when he played his first big game, an Irani trophy match in Nagpur. The hunters Bishen Singh Bedi and Erapalli Prasanna, the quarry a wiry thin Dilip Vengsarkar. The quarry turned on the pursuers, unleashing a fusillade of strokes that had everybody stunned. Vengsarkar says that he was ready when he faced up to Bedi, Pras and Ashwini Minna. Again, this is not bravado talking, but poise and confidence which comes from education in the best cricketing school—schools and *maidan* cricket. Vengsarkar says, "I met the spinners head on, I had developed my temperament at a young age." Remember, that Vegsarkar too dreamt the dream, for he too aspired to play for club and country. Sixes rained from his bat that afternoon against Bedi and Pras. This class was soon evident in the coliseums that are modern day cricket stadiums. The middle order batsman was pushed into opening for the tightness of his game and he failed. In the West Indies on the 1975-76 tour in the ill-fated Kingston Test when Clive Lloyd first unveiled his version of bodyline, the young man stood tall against Holding, Wayne Daniel, Bernard Julien and Vanburn Holder scoring 39 and 21. Vegsarkar's growth was steady and though he found himself out of the side after that, he bounced back on the tour of Australia, playing Jeff Thomson with credit. Then came the famous partnership with his role model Sunil Gavaskar at the Eden Gardens in Calcutta. India had found a worthy and accomplished batsman to carry the cross after Gavaskar and Vishwanath. The West Indian side was second string, but many of the bowlers first rate, tyros who would serve the islanders well in the future. An unfinished 344 run partnership saw Vengsarkar score the first of his 17 Test hundreds—157. Sylvester Clarke, Malcolm Marshall, Norbert Philip and Vanburn Holder made up the attack.

Vengsarkar and Gavaskar were associated in another big partnership in the same series, carrying on the *guru-shishya parampara*. At the Kotla, they added 151 runs for the second wicket with both batsmen scoring centuries. Vengsarkar had by now curbed his natural attacking instincts, though not his penchant for the cover drive or playing ramrod straight in the Vee. So, the Vengsarkar saga took root. What does Vengsarkar feel about this relationship with Gavaskar, did he ever try and imitate him consciously or unconsciously? Vengsarkar says, "I never changed or planned to change my game consciously. After my injury against England, I was dropped in the order and asked to score runs. I put my head down and started grafting, scoring two big hundreds in the Duleep Trophy. Once I began to adjust to the wickets abroad, I started playing my shots all over again." He also says that he could never bat like Gavaskar for, "Sunil was blessed with unbelievable powers of concentration. I have not seen anybody like him, technically correct and tight." Many remember a Ranji final in which both Dilip and Sunil got hundreds. Sunil batted lower down and scored a little over 200 not out, but what is notable about that innings is that Dilip, always a strokemaker, after reaching his hundred played in the air and was dropped at mid off. Instead of being more circumspect the next ball, he attacked again and was out caught off the next ball. Meanwhile, Gavaskar unperturbed continued batting. Many say that Vengsarkar changed his natural attacking flair to be more defensive, but his batting flowered not just with Gavaskar in the side, but grew in confidence after Gavaskar's retirement. They were dissimilar in their approach, the art of Zen common in essence and singlemindedness of purpose, but different in content and style.

While Vengsarkar's famous relationship with Lord's is well known—he scored three hundreds there—the changing of the guard had begun in earnest during

Gavaskar's last few years in international cricket. In the 1986 series against England which India won 2-0, Vengsarkar was in overdrive, scoring two hundreds followed quickly by another 2-0 vanquishing of Sri Lanka at home. Vengsarkar again scored two big hundreds, 157 and 166. He was undoubtedly at the peak of his prowess, with a consistency that would have done Gavaskar proud. In Gavaskar's last series against Pakistan at home, Vengsarkar was once again at the vanguard. The purple patch just got better against the West Indies where India was without Gavaskar and Vengsarkar was captain. Dadar Union had been replaced by Dadar Union as the batsman that opposition teams targeted in their crosshairs. Vengsarkar met Patrick Patterson, Winston Davis, Winston Benjamin and Courtney Walsh head on 10, 102, 51, 40 not out, 102 retired hurt. Though the following series against the West Indies in West Indies saw his form slump, Vengsarkar had established himself as one of the game's elite batsmen of his time. Vengsarkar, critical of some of his teammates on that tour says, "I can understand failure, for everyone cannot succeed, but when you run away from fast bowling, that is something I cannot tolerate. I too did not get very many runs on that tour and that probably went against me, for I lost the captaincy." Vengsarkar aggregated 6868 runs in 116 Tests with 17 hundreds. Strangely, Vengsarkar's hundreds came only in India and England, while Gavaskar scored his hundreds all round the world— 7 in West Indies, 2 in England, 1 in New Zealand, 5 in Australia and 3 in Pakistan, which meant that 18 of his hundreds had come outside India. Both were excellent all-wicket players, for they learnt their craft on the wet wickets of Kanga League.

The Ranji Trophy final (1990-91) against Haryana at the Wankhede Stadium was a high-octane humdinger. Typically Bombay, no quarter given, nor any asked for. Played in the energy-sapping heat and humidity of May, it was a showstopper all the way with Haryana winning by a coat of varnish—two runs. Haryana 522, with Deepak Sharma 199, Ajay Jadeja 94 and Chetan Sharma 98. With both sides at full strength, Bombay's reply was 410— Lalchand Rajput 74, Sanjay Patil 85 and Sachin Tendulkar 47. Kapil Dev, determined to beat Bombay, bowled 34 overs, scalping 3-54. Haryana in their second essay had trouble against Salil Ankola and Sanjay Patil, notching up only 242 with Ajay Banerjee scoring a defiant 60. It is a game that one cannot forget in a hurry. Domestic cricket on benign pitches has always seen high scoring farcical matches where first innings leads have often decided the final outcome. Flat wicket bullies have dominated in no uncertain terms. Here was a game that was stimulating; it was also a showcase of the country's top talent. While Bombay had bested Hyderabad in one of those typical high scoring games, Haryana had done the same to Bengal in the other semi-final. But this match was scheduled to go down to the wire, merely because Bombay was not going to roll over and die, only because Bombay players brought up on tradition don't roll over and die. Just as Sunil Gavaskar had made a point by batting left handed against Karnataka spinner Raghuram Bhatt (when most of his team was skittled out) in a Ranji game, now the Bombay side was out to prove a point.

The target 355 to win at five an over in 60 odd overs. Bombay in tatters at 34 for three. Dilip Vengsarkar joined by young Sachin Tendulkar counter-attacked. Vengsarkar says, "When Sachin was going for his shots and the partnership was developing, I overheard Kapil tell his teammates—don't lower your guard, Dilip and Sachin are together at the crease and anything is possible." Such was the grudging admiration for Bombay players. This comment typifies what the opposition thought about Bombay's fighting qualities and never say die approach. Sachin and Vengsarkar added 134 runs, with the former getting out for 96. But Vengsarkar found another ally in Vinod Kambli. They added 81 runs and Bombay lost a slew of wickets. Vengsarkar stood firm just as he had done against Pakistan at the Kotla in 1979 against a rampaging Sikander Bakht with a battling innings of 146 not out to take India to the brink of what would have been a famous win. Vengsarkar picked up the gauntlet, smashing 24 runs off a Yogendra Bhandari over. An unyielding and injured Vengsarkar refused to buckle, joined as he was by last man Abhey Kuruvilla. Forty-seven runs were added before Kuruvilla was run out, Vengsarkar was left like Nelson on the bridge with 139 not out. Bombay had lost by two runs. Inconsolable, he replays that match constantly in his mind.

In that same Bombay side, the next generation of batting stars were already straining at the leash. For in the quarter-final and semi-final against Delhi and Hyderabad respectively, the might of the troika's broad blades had been felt with stunning impact. Sanjay Manjrekar, Sachin Tendulkar and Vinod Kambli were in rampant form. The quarter-final played at Kotla saw Bombay coming through on the first innings lead, but by a solitary run. Manjrekar 47 and 156, Tendulkar 82 and 125, while Kambli scored 54 and 24. In the second innings, Bombay scored 719 for 8 wickets declared. A defining moment followed in the semi-final at the Wankhede stadium in the semi-final. Bombay 855 for six wickets declared. Venkatapathy Raju and Arshad Ayub were thrashed. Manjrekar smashed 377, Vengsarkar 121, Tendulkar 70, Vinod Kambli 126. In a city raised on a diet of formidable scores, it was difficult to excite hardboiled Bombayites. And surprise, surprise, there was a second innings as Bombay scored 446 for 4 wickets declared. Tendulkar 88 and Kambli 127.

Manjrekar, who was felled by Winston Benjamin in his debut Test had pedigree. Son of one of India's foremost batsmen Vijay, it was only natural that he would play for India. He says that he took to cricket like a duck takes to water, very naturally. Not only was he fascinated by the game from an early age, his father's larger than life persona had a huge influence on his cricket. From a young age, he saw cricketers coming to his house. He says, "Cricket was the best way to make one's tryst with fame, not money so much. In the Shivaji Park-Dadar area, it was the best calling card. It acted as a huge catalyst as youngsters who were seeking recognition found cricket as the best way forward." Sanjay's father Vijay and his mate Subhash Gupte triggered this change. They were at the vanguard of this change

Photo montage of Wankhede Stadium with the electronic score board and *gully* cricket in full swing, which eventually leads to the birth of many a Bombay star.

Vijay Merchant, in the Oval Test of 1946 scored a roaring 128, before being run out by Compton's quick footwork. Here he plays his favourite shot, the late cut.

Master and the Pupil: Vinoo Mankad played tutor to several left arm spinners from Bombay- Bapu Nadkarni, Paddy Shivalkar and Eknath Solkar.

Vinoo Mankad   Bapu Nadkarni

Some of the stalwarts of Bombay's triumphs:
Ramakant Desai (right corner — standing), Naren Tamhane, Polly Umrigar and
Madhav Apte (2nd, 3rd & 4th — sitting from left to right).

Bapu Nadkarni with the Bombay Ranji Trophy winning side.

A study in spin: S.P. Gupte's classic action of dragging his right foot to give him better balance enabled him to bowl his lethal leg-breaks.

Gupte shares a joke with sports journalist Sharad Kotnis, Dilip Vengsarkar and Sanjay Manjrekar.

above: Casting Vote:
Ajit Wadekar is made
captain of India by
Bombay legend Vijay
Merchant.

below: Nadkarni and
Wadekar after
savaging the bowling.

Eknath Solkar, one of the best forward short-leg fielders in the world, helped many a spinner by latching on to catches which seemed only half-chances. His contribution with the bat was also worth its weight in gold.

left to right: Chandu Borde, Wadekar, Ramakant Desai, Vijay Manjrekar, Subhash Gupte and Nari Contractor take a luncheon break.

Summer of 1971
Wadekar and Gavaskar in England.

Top: Sandeep Patil pulls Gavaskar's leg.
Left: Gavaskar and Eknath Solkar enjoy a lighter moment.
Right: Gavaskar in full flow.

amongst Maharashtrian lower middle class households. Sanjay remembers how his father never gave him any formal coaching or discussed cricket, but always believed that the boy would follow him and play for India. It was uncanny. In fact, when cricketers would visit the Manjrekar household, Vijay Manjrekar would point to his son playing in the building compound by saying, "This boy will play for India." Sanjay remembers Rohan Kanhai, Vishwanath, Gavaskar, Prasanna and Bedi visiting the house. The Manjrekars lived near Portuguese Church on Gokhale Road and during the rains when one of these stars would visit the house, Vijay would ask his young, quiet, well-behaved son Sanjay to shepherd them into the house with an umbrella. The proud father would sometimes call out to his son and make him shadow practice in front of these cricketers. The refrain was constant—this boy will definitely play for India. Young Sanjay would make all of them sign his autograph book.

And he played with a certain amount of distinction. On his return to the side after the injury, he played his first Test at Georgetown against the West Indies once again. But rain truncated the game and Manjrekar never got a bat. The next Test was at Bridgetown, Barbados. India 68 for 4 with Marshall, Curtly Ambrose, Ian Bishop and Walsh offering no respite to the Indians. With Azharuddin and Kapil Dev, Manjrekar tried to rebuild the innings. At close of play, he was still there with an unbeaten 93. But visualise this scenario. Unable to sleep, at four in the morning, Manjrekar stands practising his forward defensive stroke in front of the hotel room's mirror. The heebie-jeebies in his stomach did not allow him to sleep, tossing and turning, he could only think of the next morning. A friend's call at an unearthly hour obviously did not help. The next morning, he duly completed his hundred. Manjrekar feels he could have completed it the previous day itself what with Viv Richards bowling a few tempting donkey drops, but Manjrekar did not fall for that ruse and rolled down the shutters. The second innings and Port of Spain saw him fail, till at Kingston, Jamaica, he scored 47 and 41. Dropped for the MRF World Series and New Zealand's tour of India, Manjrekar was back for the crucial tour of Pakistan. Indian cricket had seen a lot of behind the scenes tumult, so a new captain was installed—Krish Srikkanth. Manjrekar, given an opportunity in the Irani Trophy game, failed, but still made it to Pakistan. Manjrekar asked skipper Srikkanth for the number three slot and never looked back. The whirlpool of depression was thrown out of the window, as Manjrekar became India's numero uno player in that series with over 550 runs. Wasim Akram, Waqar Younis, Imran Khan, Abdul Qadir were unable to best the Indians who returned with four draws. This remains Manjrekar's high point and though he tried to emulate his father on the tour of England, but missed a century at Old Trafford (Vijay Manjrekar scored a spirited 133 at Leeds against Alec Bedser and Fred Trueman), it was on the tour of Australia that he failed to convert the good starts into big scores. There were enough 30s, but no big scores and his agony was compounded by four run outs in the triangular series and another two in the World Cup. Vengsarkar feels that Manjrekar did not adjust well to the bounce on Australian wickets and used to get bogged down by being too defensive. Manjrekar, though, always wound his way back into the Indian side, but alas never scored a hundred at home. With 2043 runs from 37 Tests and 1994 runs in 74 one-dayers, he called it a day. All four of his hundreds came overseas—one in the Caribbean, two against Pakistan and one against Zimbabwe.

On the 1990 tour of England, Manjrekar and Tendulkar were the leading scorers with 814 and 945 runs respectively. One of the most famous battles on that tour took place when Leicester's Winston Benjamin came face to face with Manjrekar who he had given a bloody lip to on his debut. Manjrekar square drove twice, Benjamin's response three quick bouncers. Manjrekar got 66 before he got his glove to a rising ball from Allan Mullally. After the Pakistan and England tours, India and Bombay were convinced that Gavaskar's inheritor had been found. But, Manjrekar always sound and determined in the classical Bombay mould lost his way a wee bit. Even today, Manjrekar continues to comment on the game bringing his unique technical knowledge to bear while describing events on the field.

Taking the cricketing culture to the next level of competency was Vijay Manjrekar who would take his young son to Sunil Gavaskar's Hindu Colony house. Sanjay would not just be overawed, but slightly intimidated by both his father and Sunny. Sanjay says, "Sunil still speaks of my father with great respect. My father was fiercely proud of his Bombay heritage, even though as a semi-professional, he didn't play for Bombay." Sanjay Manjrekar says that there is no room for anybody showing cowardice in Bombay's cricket. Pride and passion, two enduring words which one will constantly read about in course of this treatise, remain an integral part of this culture. Sanjay will tell you that Dilip Vengsarkar and Ravi Shastri passed on this culture to people like him, "As young cricketers, we had to earn respect by being brave. Though his father, who Sanjay describes as a simple but strong individual, objected to his son opting for Dadar Union, for Sanjay it was the only choice. He joined DU because of Sunil Gavaskar and Dilip Vengsarkar. As he says, "I played for DU, because I was convinced that I would play Test cricket. Guys from lower middle class backgrounds had no other option before us but to take to cricket." Sanjay remembers being asked by a classmate in class 12, what would you do after college? My mind was focused, obviously play cricket, and I couldn't think of anything else, he says now. The discipline and will to win came from the tutelage at DU. After scoring only 34 in a club game, DU shot the opposition out for 31 to win the match.

Vasu Paranjpe played a part in Sanjay joining DU. Paranjpe was a close friend of Vijay Manjrekar's and he advised him to allow Sanjay to play for DU. An insistent Vijay wanted Sanjay to follow him at Shivaji Park Gymkhana. Paranjpe's counter was that Sanjay would become a good rummy player and not a cricketer. After an argument, where Paranjpe convinced Vijay that Sanjay would do well to play in the same DU side as Sunil Gavaskar and Dilip Vengsarkar, Manjrekar Senior relented. Sanjay Manjrekar did not receive any formal coaching; he claims a process of self-learning helped him to get to the high road. He doesn't deny the influence of Sunny and Dilip on his cricket, learning from the icons all the time.

He also remembers how Jitu Thakre and he once scored 50 odd each in a match and both were in the Bombay side to play Australia. As they got into the plane, Sunil, already seated, welcomed them with words to the effect, "Here come the new Bombay stalwarts." Both boys were tickled pink for obvious reasons. Sanjay also remembers how it was practically impossible to break into the Bombay side those days. There was even talk that he should opt for another state, but Manjrekar, destiny's child, scored six hundreds for Bombay University to seal the issue. Manjrekar says that by the time this happened, the pendulum in Indian cricket was beginning to oscillate towards Delhi that was seen as the new powerhouse. Fielding against Delhi, Manjrekar had admiration for their all round strength. He says, "In the evenings, we would discuss how Delhi had become the better side. But as soon as bowlers started coming through the ranks in Bombay, we started beating them all over again. Manjrekar was in many ways fortunate, for he played in two different eras—with Gavaskar and Vengsarkar (for the club and state) and then with the generation next—when Tendulkar and Kambli joined him. I remember going to Wankhede stadium just before that pulsating and historic Ranji final where the three of them were doing their drills. Talking to them, I sensed camaraderie and kinship as they joked, telling my colleague—do you want a picture? Sanjay remarking that they were shooting for a Fair & Lovely commercial—Vinod being before, Sanjay himself after one week of use and Sachin the finished product.

The three played well together and as Manjrekar says, once Abhey Kuruvilla, Salil Ankola and Paras Mhambrey clicked, we were once again a handful. What about the jagged edge of competition amongst the threesome, Manjrekar refutes this, saying that they were all India players and all of them scored heavily. Yes, they enjoyed intimidating opposing sides. Manjrekar says, "Barring Delhi and Karnataka, we did have some fun bullying lesser sides." He acknowledges Vengsarkar's supportive role in his early days, particularly during the transition to the Test side. He feels that Sandeep Patil played a similar role when he broke into the Bombay side. So, the Bombay relay continued.

The 1996-97 final played in Gwalior highlights this more than anything does. This was the first ever day and night final. Bombay, now Mumbai, made 630 with Amol Mazumdar scoring 144, Jatin Paranjpe 111, Manjrekar who was captain, 78 and Kambli 89. Locked in a gladiatorial contest for first innings supremacy, Delhi battled. Ajay Sharma and Ashu Dani with 176 and 178 respectively threatened to take the game away with a 313 run partnership for the third wicket. Manjrekar remembers, "Bombay had to win, we had a team meeting where I told the boys that this is going to be a very close run thing. We decided that we would defend, sweating them out, so we played to a plan." Nilesh Kulkarni did the trick, bowling a marathon spell 74.1 overs, 19 maidens, 143 runs and four wickets. Delhi was bowled out for 559. Bishen Bedi remarked,

"Delhi would have lost if the roles had been reversed." Manjrekar feels that this final among other matches once again illustrated the thinking that goes into Bombay's cricket—the paramountcy of being aware all the time, not missing anything.

In all this the role of the *gurukul* cannot be undermined, for as Vengsarkar says, "Guide and nurture the youngster so that he can be trained. When Sachin first came into the side, I was the captain. I was always keen to protect him, for he was a young boy. Yes, his batsmanship was mature, but the boy had to be shown the way. That was the Bombay culture, see that the new members are in a comfort zone. Let them play their game and thrive. For they have to stand up and be counted." And so, it was with Sachin Tendulkar…

3 | Destiny's Child

IF SUNIL GAVASKAR WAS GANDHIAN IN HIS APPROACH, implacable, placid and even obdurate at the crease, his original *shishya* Dilip Vengsarkar was considerably more free flowing. Not bogged down with opening the innings and providing the foundation to the building, Vengsarkar displayed a more attacking bent of mind. The latest member of the *gurukul* Sachin Tendulkar is diametrically opposite to both. Unarguably new age, a slugger and a streetfighter, toughened on the Shivaji Park maidan, Tendlya as he is fondly called, is an attacking phenomenon. But the phenomenon cut his teeth on the *maidan*, not Dadar Union's Matunga maidan, but Shivaji Park. As a student of New English school, Bandra, cricket from an early age, like many of his middle class peers, fascinated Tendulkar.

To pursue his dream, he joined Ramakant Achrekar's coaching scheme in Shivaji Park. But as he says, "I had to change two buses, so Achrekar Sir recommended that I change schools." The answer was Shardashram which like Balmohan Vidyamandir was in the immediate vicinity of the expanse of green. Sachin says, "My father's younger brother Suresh used to stay in Shivaji Park, so it was decided that I shift to his house to make things more convenient." His brother Ajit who also used to play cricket was instrumental in making up young Sachin's mind. There is a story that when the New English school's headmistress asked Sachin why he wanted to leave school in class seven, the young boy is reported to have said passionately, "I want to play cricket."

And so Sachin came to Shivaji Park and practiced under Achrekar's eagle eye for four years. I went and met Ramakant Achrekar to discuss the genesis of the pheno-menon. Standing in the middle of Shivaji Park, he remembered, "On this very pitch, I took Sachin's trial when he was 11 years old. He appeared to be diffident and I told his brother Ajit who was standing alongside that he is a so-so player. Then as is my practice, I shifted him to another net and from a distance, I could see that the boy had started stroking the ball ever so sweetly, middling it perfectly." Achrekar would always tell Sachin, play your natural game, don't ever curb your attacking instincts. He says, "My advice would always be to keep the ball on the turf as much as possible. What struck me about the boy during those years was his confidence. If a fellow-ward would try and pass on some advice, he would quip back to ask—'so, what are you going to teach me?'" Even as Tendulkar was practicing under Achrekar, another boy called Vinod

Kambli joined up. As Sachin says, "Vinod was fun loving but very determined. He would come all the way from Kanjur Marg to practice." This sentence from Sachin throws into stark relief the gritty nature of Bombay's youth, for they want to succeed because they understand that a whole new world of opportunities is available through cricket. It gives a peep into the psyche of boys like Manjrekar, Tendulkar, Kambli and even Pravin Amre who played briefly for India as well (he scored a fine 103 on his debut against South Africa in 1992-93 in Durban). Achrekar, an opening batsman and wicket-keeper was always a difficult bat to dislodge during his time when he played for New Hind and State Bank of India. A contemporary of Vijay Manjrekar and Subhash Gupte, he too grew up in the *gullies* of Shivaji Park playing tennis ball cricket. Achrekar Sir came into prominence as the potter who while playing with clay left indelible imprints through the achievements of pupils like Sachin, Kambli, Amre, Chandu Pandit *et al*.

Achrekar's father, V.B. Achrekar, used to play alongside Vijay Manjrekar's father for New Hind Sporting. Achrekar never played for Bombay, for he had to compete with the likes of Naren Tamhane and Chandu Patankar. What prompted Achrekar to take to coaching? It was a freak occurrence. In the mid-1960s, Achrekar was the secretary of New Hind. To organise the club's cricketing gear, Achrekar went to India Sports House one evening. Even while chatting with the owner, Suresh Shastri, a wetnose on the greens walked into the shop. The India Sports House owner thought that young Shastri had talent and hence, he asked Achrekar to take him under his wing. This is when

Achrekar started to coach. He would chaperone Shastri to the nets, honing his skills. The president of Arya Samaj, Mithailal Singh, whose son was also practicing at the nets was highly impressed with Achrekar's demeanor. Singh asked Achrekar to accept money for coaching his son. Achrekar flatly refused, claiming that all he wanted was Rs 50 per month towards conveyance expenses. Thereafter, he turned coach for Dayanand Balak Vidyalaya which traversed to the final of the Giles Shield where they lost to Balmohan who had Sandeep Patil in their ranks.

His coaching began to pick up momentum and he became a regular at Azad maidan where he started instructing Sassanian CC players. The albatross's wing-span grew larger as Hindi Vidya Bhavan also approached him. Another inflection point came when he switched to Shardashram in the early 1970s. But this association with Shardashram, the Arya Samaj school ended soon. Those days three inter-school tournaments used to be played—North Bombay schools, Giles and Harris Shields. Achrekar's school was reaching the final of all three and the expenditure incurred was proving exorbitant. Mithailal Singh also had to relinquish his post due to the same reason. Over the years, many of his wards have played Ranji Trophy—Padam Shastri, Suresh Shastri, Sharad Rao, Balwinder Singh Sandhu, Ravi Kulkarni, Ramnath Parkar, Lalchand Rajput, Tendulkar, Amre, Kambli and Chandu Pandit. Incidentally, Amre was related to Ramnath Parkar. Amre's father moved from Carpenter Street to Shivaji Park so that his son could practice without a care in the world.

What was the secret of his success? He says, "I always looked at kids in the 7-11 age group because I felt that a 12-year-old was too old. If the boy shows promise and talent, then I make him bat in two or three nets one after another. And, then they have to play matches, for there is nothing like competition." While practice, he felt made them perfect, he would write the errors creeping into their game in a little book that he maintained. After practice, he would call them individually and read out the mistakes so that they could improve. Instinct, approach and strokes should never be tampered with, according to him. Sachin's pronounced bottom handed grip was one such thing that Achrekar felt should be changed, but when Sachin insisted, he allowed him to continue with it. Achrekar will tell you that when Kambli first came to him in the rains, he was quick to notice the boy's marvellous ball sense. He says, "The moment he would see a half volley, he would lift it unhesitatingly. I used to wonder why Vinod batted like this, till I visited his home. There I saw a gap between the two buildings where he used to play his cricket. Since it was a long, narrow corridor, the idea was that if you lifted the ball to the first floor, it would yield you two runs and lifting the ball to the second floor meant that four runs would accrue."

"My pupils should play more and more" is Achrekar's mantra. He says, "The road is long and arduous and I never applaud their performances for I am never satisfied." Achrekar, a coach for many years came into the spotlight when the terrible twins—Tendulkar and Kambli—began to blitz one and all in school cricket. The Harris Shield became their very own domain. Gavaskar and Rege were unable to win the Harris Shield for St Xavier's, but the salt and pepper combine of Sachin and Kambli won it for Shardashram (English). In fact, Shardashram Vidyamandir won the title four straight times between 1985-86 and 1988-89 and with the momentum provided by the duo won again four times in a row between 1991-92 and 1994-95. Ajit Agarkar captained Shardashram to victory in 1992-93. In fact such was the domination of Shardashram in those days that the final would often be against Shardashram (Marathi) which lost five finals to their English counter-parts. Records were torpedoed and the duo began to walk the path of greatness as far back as February, 1988. Playing at Sassanian on Azad maidan, Shardashram smashed a score of 748 against St Xavier's with Sachin 329 and Kambli 349 running up a partnership of 664 runs. Xavier's, mute spectators to the whole *tour de force* performance collapsed for 154 in reply with Kambli taking 6-37. One of the hapless Xavier's bowlers who bore the brunt of this attack was Sairaj Bahutule, who went for 182 runs in 27 overs.

Tendulkar was the lord of all he surveyed in this arena. Another triple hundred, 346 not out, against Anjuman-e-Islam confirmed his growing reputation while Kambli smashed 224 against Anjuman the following year. Sachin threw in a 276 for good measure as well. George Robert Canning or Lord Harris as he was better known would have been proud of the two youngsters. After all, the Harris Shield is over 100 years old in Mumbai. Tendulkar remembers how during one of those partnerships with Kambli, while they were batting at Cross maidan, "Vinod had dropped his bat and was flying a kite. Achrekar Sir who used to always jot down points had written Vinod kite. Once the session concluded, he was furious, slapping Kambli, telling him to be serious." Tendulkar says that if he missed a practice due to unavoidable circumstances, Achrekar Sir would come around and pick him up on his scooter.

His memories are particularly sharp about those formative years. As he says, "I used to play two matches a day at Shivaji Park and Azad maidan. The discipline instilled in me by Achrekar Sir has really helped me. He provided me with support and was always there to guide me. Initially he tried to change my grip, but the two of us discussed it with Ajit, my brother and decided to stick to the original grip." He used to bat in one net after another till it came to the fifth net that was the exclusive preserve of the seniors. By then young Sachin would be tired, but the challenge of not getting out would make Sachin give that extra. Achrekar would keep a one rupee coin on the stumps for the bowler to get if he got Sachin out. Such was the young boy's determination that he would ensure that he didn't get out, so as to keep the coin. When Sachin wasn't given the Mumbai Cricket Association Best Junior Cricketer of the Year award, he received a missive from one Sunil Manohar Gavaskar. The signed missive basically explained to Sachin that he shouldn't lose heart, after all he (Sunil) had also missed out on the same award and in his later career, he (Sunil) hadn't done so badly. Once again this shows how the relay of Bombay batting was being run. Encourage the youngsters so that they take the battle forward!

Then at 14, Sachin was picked to play for Bombay against Baroda. Sandeep Patil was the manager and he along with Kiran Mokashi who was a member of the Bombay side saw to it that the boy had a smooth transition into the big bad world of first class cricket. Sachin says that even when he was a member of the Bombay under-15 side, he would be constantly looking at the Ranji side that would be practicing on the same ground. As is well known, it didn't take Sachin very long to make the cut. He was the highest scorer in his very first season, with an aggregate of 583 runs. When he was picked to play for the Rest of India in the Irani Trophy game against Delhi, he came through with flying colours 42 and 100. Delhi had a fine attack— Sanjeev Sharma, Madan Lal, Atul Wassan, Manoj Prabhakar and Maninder Singh. The rest lost the game, but Sachin slugged it out till the end. On 92 not out, when he ran out of partners, with an injured Gursaran Singh in the pavilion, it was Raj Singh Dungarpur who requested Gursaran to go out and bat. Sachin managed to get the hundred with an injured Gursaran at the other end. This was his first and a great cricketing odyssey was underway.

On his first tour of Pakistan, that was also his baptism into international cricket, Tendulkar did not flinch for a moment. On that tour, Tendulkar met fire with fire not once but twice, and this is the stuff that legends are made of. Tendulkar says, "When you share a dressing room and play for India, a sense of pride and self respect is uppermost. I have never liked being a loser. When I was hit on my face by a Waqar Younis snorter at Sialkot, derisive comments about being a *bachcha* could be heard. I misjudged the length and lost the ball against the sightscreen. It didn't feel nice, what with blood flowing from my nose, but I couldn't leave the field for the side wasn't doing well." In your face attitude, so typical for a Mumbaikar, but for one so young was truly amazing. Sachin says that he knew in the immediate aftermath there was going to be pain, but the ice helped and he regained his composure quickly. The Maharashtrian in Sachin refused to back down. In the background, he could hear comments like—Waqar, hit him again, but he wasn't overawed. It was an important period of play, two more bouncers followed in rapid succession. Sachin says, "I told myself, I want to thrash this bowler." No fear, no emotion as the next three balls were calmly dispatched to the boundary to end an eventful over. Tendulkar had passed the litmus test, scoring 57. Tendulkar scored 15, 59, 8, 41, 35, 57 to announce his arrival on the world stage. Against Abdul Qadir in what turned into an exhibition game, there was uninhibited hitting after the leg spinner taunted him repeatedly. Sachin smote him all over that day to make another announcement to the cricket comity. Sachin says, "I had to attack, we needed 40 runs in two overs and I thought, there is no point in hanging around."

Named after Sachin Dev Burman, that melodious music director of the 1950s and 1960s, Sachin is more of a hard rocker. By instinct, an attacking player, he has played more or less the same way since his early days at Shardashram or Shivaji Park Youngsters or CCI. Cricket might be a team game played by 22 individuals, but within the bigger battle, there are always interesting and appetising sideshows. Sachin says, "Yes, sometimes it is premeditated, but my game hasn't changed at all. I love to attack and get on top of the bowler." What about his duels with the mingy Glen McGrath in recent times? He says, "He is an aggressive bowler and I am an attacking batsman. I have to get the better of the exchanges." Not only does Sachin walk the walk, but he also talks and talk, for he has been in innumerable scrapes. What is most interesting about him is his photographic memory; he will be able to give details about every single mode of dismissal over the years.

In the Ranji Trophy, a chorus often goes out that Mumbai is Sachin Tendulkar and without him, it is not possible to win the Ranji trophy. The evidence certainly points in that direction. In 1999-2000 when Mumbai won the Ranji Trophy under Sameer Dighe's stewardship, it was Sachin who just laid everybody low with some astonishing batting. Does he raise the mental bar or psyche himself up for a particular contest? Tendulkar feels that he plays the same way all the time, just as Gavaskar says that his mind was on high alert, whatever the match. Scoring runs is the key. In the Ranji semi-final, Tamil Nadu scored 485 after being 149 for 4 with Robin Singh (183 not out) and Hemang Badani (162) threatening to take the match away from Mumbai. Ajit Agarkar bowled his heart out taking 4-83. Dighe 55 and Kambli 75 supported Sachin Tendulkar who played a blinder, taking it upon himself to win the match for Mumbai. Let Sachin tell us, "It was touch and go. All nine fielders were on the boundary line and I had Santosh Saxena and Abhey Kuruvilla for company. As it happened, the last two wickets added 43 runs and I scored all of them. It was one of the most thrilling moments of my career." Sachin scored a career best 233 not out and the shot which brought Mumbai the lead is embedded in the recesses of my memory. A cover drive bisecting point and extra cover hit so hard that a fielder like Robin Singh who was on the fence couldn't cut it off, even after a despairing dive. Mumbai reached 490 and a dispirited Tamil Nadu side just threw in the towel. Bowled out for 171 in the second innings, Mumbai won by eight wickets and the flame of Sachin's genius burned brighter. The ghost of the nail biting 1990-91 final against Haryana had been exorcised. Sachin can tell you till this day that he was caught by Ajay Jadeja off Yogendra Bhandari's bowling for 96 in that ill-fated run chase. Anyway, the final was against Hyderabad, captained in a Ranji final for the first time by Mohammed Azharuddin at the Wankhede stadium. Mumbai managed 376 in their first essay with the old firm of Tendulkar 53 and Kambli 108 holding forth. Paras Mhambrey pitched in with 75 as Venkatapathy Raju took 4-110. Hyderabad replied with a modest 195; only Azhar standing tall with 76. Mumbai once again saw Tendulkar 128 and Kambli 56 leading the way to put together a total of 409. Was the issue beyond Hyderabad? Well almost, only Laxman with 111 coped with Rajesh Pawar who scalped 7-103. Mumbai had won for the first time since Manjrekar's side had won at Gwalior in 1996-97. The partying at a Mahim pub (not far from Shivaji Park) Scottish Arms continued till the wee hours of the morning.

Tendulkar as a boy idolised Vivian Richards and Sunil Gavaskar. He says, "When I used to practice in the nets, I would like to take the ball on the bat the way Richards would do in videos that I had watched of him. Sunil Gavaskar's deeds were used by me for inspiration." But the unmistakable arrogance and swagger of Richards rubs off on Sachin's batting. There is no arrogance, nor is there any swagger in Sachin's batting, but the attacking intent and the strong will to subjugate the bowler is there for all to see. He says, "Yes, I want to dominate the bowling. Remember that cricket is also a contest between the bowler and the batsman. Though I have never consciously singled out any bowler, I like to score runs all the time. That is my job, my occupation." And he agrees that there are times, when he changes his game after analysing the situation, telling himself, "Today is the day to counter-attack." All those present at Mumbai's Wankhede stadium during the 1996 World Cup game, the first under floodlights, will vouch for Sachin's comment. Australia 258 and India's repartee a damp squib. Glen McGrath bowls three successive maidens to Jadeja; Damien Fleming keeps it tight at the other end. Ajay Jadeja and local boy Vinod Kambli go quickly and quietly into the night. McGrath has now bowled four overs for four runs, when the floodgates open, the dykes burst and Tendulkarmania is unleashed. Sachin will tell you that he just played his shots, but all of us who saw the mayhem will remember it for a long time. It was a calculated assault and the target was McGrath. Pulling him over the infield, then hooking him off his chin and smashing him through the covers, Tendulkar was taking the fight to the enemy camp. Fleming was cut and then driven to long off. The crowd was going bananas, screaming their heads off— Sachin, Sachin, Sachin was the cry. Just as a crowd gathered to see the little big fella against Tamil Nadu and Hyderabad in the Ranji matches later, those who congregated at the Wankhede that evening had come to pay obeisance to the master. Frenetic is the only way to describe his innings—Warne was sent packing over the boundary, and sliced for four of the next ball, a trifle dangerously. This wasn't the Bombay style of batsmanship, this was contemporary Mumbai of the nineties—rash and dazzling, an array of strokes which left you wondering what the alchemist would produce next. Mark Waugh though had the last laugh, getting Sachin stumped by Healy for 90 off 84 balls. But Sachin confesses that when he plays for Mumbai, he plays more freely for international pressures are that much more stifling.

His relationship with Sanjay Manjrekar and Vinod Kambli remains enduring, even as he has outlasted both in the combat zone that is international cricket. He says, "The two have offered yeoman service to Mumbai and Indian cricket. I don't think they have failed, it is just a set of circumstances that have affected them. They were both tremendous players who have given immense joy to a lot of people. We have had some great times together. We should remember what they have done and not what they could have done." Sachin doesn't want to discuss the mountains that he wants to climb, for it is still halfway house for this enterprising batsman. There are definite targets that he has set himself. Greater consistency and bigger scores may well be something that he has decided for the second part of his cricketing career. Gavaskar thinks

Sachin may well become the first batsman to score 15,000 Test runs and 45 hundreds.

Madhav Mantri recounts how on the tour of England in 1990 (Mantri was manager), Sachin scored 68 and 119 at Old Trafford. The morning after the 100, he came to Mantri's room and sat at his feet and asked how he had played. Always humble and simple, on the same tour, he once again went to Mantri's room after he heard that he was being rested for the tour game against Derbyshire. Mantri says, "The boy very simply dropped hints of how he had played English bowlers, right through the tour, but now was keen to play some West Indians." The reason was clearly that he wanted to duel with Ian Bishop who was playing for Derby. Excelling while learning has been his forte and the 105 not out against Bishop and Derby went a long way in completing his cricketing education. During the innings at Old Trafford against England, Tendulkar gave enough glimpses of his breathtaking power and repertoire of strokes. India trying to save the match were 127 for 5, but Tendulkar, all steel, fought back undaunted and undeterred, adding an unfinished 160 runs with Manoj Prabhakar. This was Sachin's first Test hundred and the seamless migration from boy to manhood had been completed during the innings.

Ravi Shastri who has been following Sachin's career with great interest and played alongside him says, "I was playing for Glamorgan, in England when *The Times* correspondent asked me about the new boy Tendulkar. I remember telling them that he had been sent by God to play cricket and entertain people, when he finished, he would just walk into the sunset leaving millions unsatiated, but at the same time with memories to cherish." Now, he reckons the time has come for Sachin to actively voice his opinions on the game. Shastri, never one to mince words, feels that Sachin should be proactive and not let himself be pushed around. It is time for the young man to take a stand, says Shastri. If this quality blossoms, Shastri says, India will have a ruthless future batsman.

Already, one can sense a change in Sachin. While batting, he is seen coaxing his younger partners in the course of partnerships. He is talking to his partner, giving them tips on tightening their game, even during the heat of the game. That means the introvert is beginning to step out of his shadow. Most recently, one saw him talking to Badani—play straight came the call from the non-striker's end. At 28 and the seniormost player in the side, Tendulkar may revel in his new role. Particularly in Mumbai cricket, Sachin is the shining star, a role model, a mega star, and an iconoclast who has come through the mill. As he told me before going to South Africa "Mumbai cricket is alive and well. I don't subscribe to the theory that Mumbai cricket is bedevilled with problems. We are still producing good cricketers; yet consistency is proving a damper. Remember that other states have also raised their game considerably. The most important drawback is that our bench strength is very weak. This used to be the Mumbai juggernaut's biggest strength. The talent pools are very much there, all some of these boys need is guidance. I want to spend time with some of them like Vinayak Mane, talk to them, to make the deeds of our hoary past reverberate in their memory recesses. We are still a dangerous side and the side that every team in India aspires to beat." It is all about cranking up the game. Many in Mumbai, including Sachin, feel that Amol Mazumdar could have been the next batting star out of the city, but he was hard done by selectorial policies, even as lesser players from other states were preferred. Sachin says, how could you have ignored a man who scored 100s in the Ranji quarter-final, semi-final and final in the same year. Sachin thinks that the Mumbai Ranji team is working very hard and it is a matter of time before the jigsaw is complete. Of course, his presence will lift them as it always does, but international commitments beckon. Mumbai cricket is all about heroes. Kids on the *maidans* reliving memories, channeling their thoughts and actions to become better players. The 'I'—inspiration factor may well become the 'T'—Tendulkar factor in Mumbai cricket. Dilip Sardesai reckons that Sachin is the greatest Bombay batsman ever. Between Sachin and Kambli, he says, "Both were born with the talent, one is perfect and the other not so. Both have served their state and country well."

Tendulkar, many believe is now stepping into the prime zone of his career. His achievements will only help pump prime the level of the game in the city.

4 | Bombay, *circa* 1970

BOMBAY ALWAYS DOMINATED THE MAKE UP OF INDIAN teams. In fact, Khandu Rangnekar who travelled to Australia in 1948 with Lala Amarnath's side to play the Invincibles would always say that Bombay should have two sides representing it in the Ranji Trophy. Such was the strength both on the field and in the reserves. Starting with Madhav Apte leading the side to victory in 1958-59, Bombay won 15 straight titles in an astonishing run. The captaincy was shared around—Apte led in two of these wins, Polly Umrigar in three, Bapu Nadkarni in three, Manohar Hardikar in two, Ajit Wadekar in four and Sudhir Naik in 1970-71 when five frontline Bombay players were donning India colours on the famous twin tour victories of the West Indies and England. Never was this strength and domination thrown into starker contrast as on those twin tours. Even on the earlier twin tours of Australia and New

Zealand when Tiger Pataudi was the captain, Bombay players were present in the side—Farokh Engineer, Dilip Sardesai, Ajit Wadekar, Russi Surti (very much Bombay bred, a Parsi Cyclists regular, but playing for Gujarat), Bapu Nadkarni and Umesh Kulkarni. The first five were regulars, while Kulkarni and Ramakant Desai traded places.

For the 1969-70 return visit of the Kiwis and the Australians, chairman of the selection committee Vijay Merchant began a churning process which saw the advent of fresh faces into the Indian team. The young Turks handpicked by Merchant replaced the old guard. Chetan Chauhan, Ajit Pai, Ambar Roy, K.S. Indrajitsinhji, Ashok Mankad, Eknath Solkar, Ashok Gandotra, Subroto Guha, Gundappa Vishwanath, Mohinder Amarnath were the young players used in the eight Tests. Tiger once told me that he couldn't understand whether Merchant wanted the side to win or lose, so much chopping and changing was going on that nobody was sure of his place. Anyway some of these boys went onto serve Indian cricket very well— Solkar, Vishwanath, Chauhan, Mohinder, Mankad while the others faded away into the twilight zone. As these boys faded, so did the age of the Nawab and many who had played for India alongside him. Mansur Ali Khan, the erstwhile Nawab of Pataudi was cast out with the chairman's casting vote and an era appeared to have ended in Indian cricket.

Merchant from Bombay had made the Bombay captain Ajit Wadekar captain of India. While Polly Umrigar had led India in the past, as had Contractor (another Bombay-bred player who used to turn out for Gujarat), Bombay had not

had an India captain for many years. Though the twin tours
saw Merchant relenting and giving Wadekar some of the
senior pros from the previous regime. Men like M L
Jaisimha, Salim Durrani, Abbas Ali Baig were still around,
but the fountainhead of youth unveiled by Merchant was
all-pervasive. One Sunil Gavaskar and his appetite for runs
had also impressed Merchant and hence he too made the
touring party. If one does a back of the envelope calculation
of what the Bombay boys achieved on those twin tours of
the Caribbean and England, the results will show that they
practically won both series for India. In the first Test, it was
'Sardee' maan—Dilip Sardesai who was in the trenches,
combating the West Indies, ably supported by Eknath
Solkar. At 75 for 6, the duo came together and taking the
score to 212, were separated. Sardesai 212 and Solkar 61. In
the fourth Test, there was an action replay. Sardesai 150 and
Solkar 65, who put together a stand of 189 runs, rescued
India teetering at 70 for 6. Ashok Mankad and Sunil
Gavaskar joined hands in the second Test at Port of Spain,
missing the first as a result of injuries. Mankad, Gavaskar,
Sardesai and Solkar scored impressively on that tour.
Though Wadekar had a miserable time in the West Indies,
he too got into the thick of things in a low scoring series
against England.

It was fairy tale for Sardesai as he presented a broad
blade to everything that the West Indians threw at him. At
Barbados airport, he was asked by immigration—Sardee
maan, anything to declare? Such was the man's confidence
on that tour that he said—Runs maan, only runs! If Sardesai
made it to the twin tours, it was merely at the insistence of

the newly installed captain, Ajit Wadekar. Similarly, Wadekar plumped for a young man called Gavaskar, and it was a meeting of minds, for Merchant too was impressed with the St Xavier's lad. Wadekar says, "There are a lot of stories about Vijay Merchant and how he was vindictive, but I always found him businesslike and he supported me to the hilt. Moreover, he had a human face and his work for the underpriviliged is well known." Wadekar goes on to say, "When Merchant picked me to captain India, people thought I wasn't mature, but he would always say: Wadekar will get us results."

Ajit Wadekar was a reluctant cricketer, but he certainly got results for India, both as captain and in his avatar of manager many years later. Once he took to the game, he went right to the top. A product of Shivaji Park, Ajit Wadekar had the most unusual initiation into the game. In his case, it was hell hath no fury as a boy scorned. Born and brought up near the *maidan*, Wadekar went to C.L. Boys High School where he never played cricket. Since he performed well academically, he got admission at Elphinstone College. Elphinstone, in fact had an excellent cricket team with Vasu Paranjpe and Baloo Gupte as its fulcrum. Baloo Gupte was Wadekar's neighbour and as such they would travel together by bus to the college. Wadekar says that Baloo asked him in the bus whether he wanted to be 12th man for the college team. It was *circa* 1958 and the 12th man got an allowance of Rs three per day. Wadekar joined the team and after practicals would land up for practice. But Madhav Mantri was the coach and a real stickler and he brooked no nonsense from anybody. So,

Wadekar was always made to do three to four rounds. Wadekar says, "I had no interest in cricket whatsoever. I actually went to the principal and requested him to let me come late for cricket practice." However, he refused and asked Wadekar to opt for Arts. Then fate intervened.

Aru Wagh from Khar fell sick just before the inter-collegiate final against Siddarth and Wadekar who was 12th man was drafted in. Minutes before the start of the match, nobody could find Wadekar. The match was at CCI and Elphinstone were fielding with 10 men. Ajit Wadekar was in the canteen, while his side was getting a pasting. Later Elphinstone captain Arvind Apte found him in the canteen and gave Wadekar a tongue lashing. A very hurt Wadekar told Apte that he would show him that he could be a good cricketer as well. Wadekar joined Ruia college where Nandu Raje was the captain. College, a quick dosa at Mansi and rigorous practice with P.K. Kamath between 2.30 and 7.00 p.m. became a daily regimen. The very same year Wadekar played for the college and then Bombay University. Smashing the inter-university record in 1959, Wadekar had arrived. The same year, he played for Bombay that was being led by Polly Umrigar. The side replete with stars—G.S. Ramchand, Madhav Apte, Manohar Hardikar, Nanu Pai, Naren Tamhane, Bapu Nadkarni, Baloo Gupte, Ghulam Guard, Farokh Engineer and Sudhakar Adhikari. Wadekar and Hoshi Amroliwala were fighting for a spot on this team.

Wadekar says, "I hadn't even played for SPG in the Kanga league." It was only after he met Vijay 'Tatt' Manjrekar that he played for SPG. Yet, Wadekar now says that it was destined that he would play. For as he says, "Cricket was in my blood. After all I was born on that soil." Wadekar, Hardikar, Ramakant Desai, Ramakant Achrekar had played enough *gully* cricket earlier in the lanes of Shivaji park. Wadekar says that all the boys would contribute one rupee each and play what was called a Shield. The man who thought of becoming an engineer became India's cricket captain by sheer accident. Yet, Manjrekar was Wadekar's idol. Wadekar remembers Manjrekar's constant encouragement. Tatt would always tell him that he should strive to make the Indian team. As a left hander who had a penchant for big scores and flashing strokeplay, it was only a matter of time that Wadekar would begin to idolise Garfield Sobers.

And when Sobers led the West Indies in 1966-67, Wadekar made his debut at the Brabourne Stadium. A humble Wadekar now recounts, "Sobers saw me in the nets. He saw that my shoes were torn. He spoke to me for a few moments and asked me my shoe size." A couple of days later, he actually turned up at Wadekar's Shivaji Park house with a pair of shoes. Wadekar cannot forget that gesture just as he cannot forget how Sobers came to the airport to receive him when the Indian team landed in the West Indies in 1970-71. Wadekar had grown up quickly in the big bad world of international cricket for he told Sobers—you are my role model, but on the field you are my enemy.

The air was thick with cricket in Shivaji Park and Wadekar's inspiration were Manjrekar and Madhu mama (Sandeep Patil's father). Wadekar says, "Once we beat Parsi Cyclists in the Talim Shield final and this was significant, for Behram Irani was hot property those days with the ball. Madhu mama, so happy with the outcome took everybody home that day for *puri* and *shrikand*. Another time, the Kanga league was on and it was pouring cats and dogs, but I still took a bus to Hindu Gymkhana thinking that the match would be played. The club secretary's retort was— have you got your swimming trunks?" That was the spirit with which the game was played those days. Wadekar says the ethos with which the game was played was different. He gives the example of a SPG vs DU match at Matunga Gymkhana. Nana Mantri was well set and Wadekar asked Ramakant 'Tiny' Desai to feed his strength, the square cut. Wadekar stood at cover point when Mantri essayed a rasping cut which he pouched. Even as Mantri walked past Wadekar, he said—well held. Another time, Wadekar went at number eight against Saurashtra with Bombay precariously perched at 100 for 6. Engineer was batting at the other end, and Wadekar got out to the last ball. In the dressing room, Polly Umrigar who was captain gave him the firing of his life. Wadekar now says that one doesn't forget these incidents and tries to pass on the same stuff to the next generation. Many say that Ajit Wadekar was a murderer of bowling in the Ranji Trophy, such was the power of his strokeplay. Paranjpe in particular remembers the speed at which Wadekar used to score his runs. Once playing at Rajkot, Bombay was 137-7 with Ramesh Divecha bowling with the new ball. Wadekar just launched into Divecha, smashing him for five boundaries. Another time, in a Ranji final against Rajasthan, Wadekar scored 285 against Vinoobhai and Subhash Gupte.

Wadekar also remembers the DU-SPG battles or the Ruia vs Siddarth matches where people would throng to watch the game. Wadekar believes that a strong sense of history has always guided Bombay players, but concurrently a work ethic which comes from lack of grounds and proper infrastructure made boys like him try that much harder. Wadekar says such was the popularity of the game those days that Ram Joshi (Bombay University vice chancellor), Shiv Sena supremo Balasaheb Thackeray and Shiv Sena leader Manohar Joshi were regulars at SPG-DU games. If Wadekar was blessed by somebody upstairs, then the man who kept India in business in the West Indies—Dilip Sardesai—was a hardworking cricketer. If Wadekar was part of a Ranji winning side for 15 of his 16 years, then Sardesai never saw defeat in domestic cricket. The first two years, Sardee was in the reserves and the next eleven, he was an integral member of the team. As Sardesai says, "After I retired, they lost for the first time in 15 years."

If it was pre-ordained that Wadekar would lead India to three successive series wins, then similarly, it was destined that Sardesai, an outsider in Bombay cricket would win two of those series with his own bat. Sardesai came to Bombay from Margao in Goa to study at Wilson College. Trained by M.S. Naik, Sardesai soon began to make waves in college and university cricket. Batting against Baroda University, Sardesai compiled a neat hundred in front of Vijay Hazare, then chairman of the all-India university selection committee. Next stop was a game for the Combined Universities against Pakistan in 1960-61 where Sardesai scored 85, facing up to Fazal Mahmood and Mahmood

Hussain. Sardesai remembers that such was the strength of the Bombay team that when he made his debut for Bombay, it was batting at number seven against Rajasthan in the Ranji final and the game got over in three days. Another time, at the Brabourne Stadium, Mysore scored 380 in the final and began to suffer from delusions of grandeur. The president of the Mysore association Dr Thimapiah flew to Bombay the next day thinking that at last Bombay's suzerainty over the Trophy was to be broken. In a celebratory mood, he was stunned to find that Bombay overcame that score for the loss of just one wicket, with Wadekar scoring a triple century and Sardesai getting a hundred.

When Sardesai arrived from Goa, he played for National CC (a club, which dominates A division Kanga League today, having won six times since 1993, coached as it is presently by Sudhir Naik). But while scoring an unbeaten 80 out of Wilson's 120 against Siddarth, he got membership in P.G. Hindu Gymkhana almost overnight. This was at the behest of Vinoo Mankad who had watched his innings. Sardesai says, "Vinoobhai had a knack of spotting talent. When I used to bat in the Hindu Gym nets, Vinoobhai would stand next to me and constantly reprimand me by hitting me on my side if I was doing something wrong. Vinoobhai would always concentrate on two or three boys who he thought deserved attention." Bombay's cricketing ethos is what stands out, according to Sardesai, with one great name giving way to another, passing on tips. If Umrigar learnt from Mantri, then Gavaskar learnt from Wadekar and so on. Sardesai remembers the camaraderie that existed in the old days, travelling by train and the team gatherings in the evenings in the captain's room. He says, "Once while part of the Bombay University team led by Sharad Diwadkar, the whole side were playing cards in the dead of the night. We heard somebody approaching the door and quickly shut off the lights. As it happened, manager Prabhu Desai was outside. When Desai switched on the lights, he found, everybody was curled up holding cards. It was hilarious!"

Two things have been forgotten by the present generation of Bombay players, according to Sardesai. He reckons that a critical facet of Bombay's batsmen was that they attached a price tag to their wicket, whatever the occasion. More importantly, they were being pushed to perform constantly and consistently, for there were players on the bench who were waiting for the big opportunity to seal their places. Sardesai believes that the cutting edge of battle in domestic cricket has also eroded. He feels that the Bombay-Karnataka battles were gladiatorial contests. He loved using his feet to the spinners and remembers scoring three hundreds against them. Sardesai's soulmate was Ramakant Desai as they played alongside each other for ACC, Bombay and India. Sardesai says, "Such was our dominance that Rajasthan lost seven finals and they had players of the calibre of Vinoo Mankad, Russi Surti, Vijay Manjrekar, Subhash Gupte, Salim Durrani and Hanumant Singh turning out for them. It was our mindset that was the differentiator." In one of those finals, which Bombay

polished off in a little over two and a half days, captain
Polly Umrigar didn't allow his team members to eat the
biryani which was being served at lunch time, till the game
was wrapped up.

The cosmopolitan nature of the city never allowed
Bombay boys to get involved in the regional biases that
crept into the Indian side during that era. Sardesai and
Gavaskar both remember how they were always open
with the other players while touring. Particularly on the
1970-71 twin tours where they were being invited all the
time by Indians residents in the West Indies and England.
But Gavaskar says the others never showed the same level
of reciprocity. He says, "I think this came from the
openness that Bombay players were used to, coming as
they did from an open culture which always existed in
Bombay's cricket and on a larger canvas in the city which
was a true melting pot."

Take Eknath Solkar, son of a groundsman at Hindu
Gymkhana, but fielder non-pareil. Discovered and tutored
by Vinoo Mankad. In fact, a common thread ran through
the formative years of several Bombay players. That thread
was Vinoobhai. Solkar used to attend the L.R. Tairsee nets
at Hindu Gym along with Vinoobhai's two sons Ashok and
Atul and he was completely in awe of the legendary all-
rounder who he wanted to model himself on. Ekky says,
"Vinoobhai was different in his approach as a coach, he
would not tinker with your game. I had this awkward
stance, but Vinoobhai encouraged me to improvise. He was
an advocate and votary of positive thinking and playing
one's natural game. Boldness was his forte." Solkar

remembers the time that he was playing for Mafatlal where his son Ashok was the captain. Physical training used to be conducted every morning at CCI and Ashok Mankad would insist that Ekky do 16 rounds. But Ekky found that he could do only 7 or 8. So Ashok complained to Vinoobhai, but his complaint was rejected for the latter told him that not only was Solkar fit, but also he had the requisite talent to perform at the highest level. Solkar was once slapped by Vinoobhai for bowling medium pace, because he thought that Solkar was a far better spinner. As a premier spinner of his time, he encouraged Solkar to flight the ball, utilise the crease and to bowl the armer from the corner. Moreover, he would always tell Solkar that he should field well off his own bowling. Vinoobhai was the biggest influence on Solkar's career and circumstances forced him to open the bowling for India because there was a surfeit of left arm spinners.

In 1965, Solkar captained Indian schoolboys against the English and played under him people like Mohinder Amarnath, Dhiraj Parsanna, Ashok Gandotra and Ramesh Nagdev. At a young age, Solkar was drafted into the Bombay side, when chairman of the Bombay selection committee Khandu Rangnekar gave him an opportunity Hardikar was captain and Bombay played Saurashtra at Jamnagar. The side had Madhav Apte, Sharad Diwadkar, Ajit Wadekar, Sardesai, Farokh Engineer, Baloo Gupte and Bapu Nadkarni among others. Playing alongside these players wasn't just a thrill, but on education. Gavaskar says that when the team would travel by train, the younger players would be perched on the upper berths. They would listen intently to the stories of valour and courage and this was most invigorating. Two stories that Gavaskar still recounts are of Ramakant Desai and Bapu Nadkarni. He says, "Desai always had Hanif Mohammed's number. Whenever Hanif would come in to bat, Tiny would bowl a bouncer and more often than not snare him fending the rising ball. Bapuji's great story was when Trueman hit him and there was talk of getting an X-ray done. Trueman's big joke: why do you need to go to hospital, you can hold up Bapu against the sun and take an X-ray. When this story was being told, Bapuji would get agitated saying—so what, at least I held out and played."

Players went through this toughening process. And that turned them into tougher players at the international level. A case in point is Solkar batting at Barbados in that famous stand with Sardesai when the ball went out of shape. Sobers and the umpire were conferring when Sardesai asked Solkar to check what was going on? Solkar went boldly, but with deference asked Sobers, "Sir, can I see the ball? Sobers replied yes, it is because of your snicks that the ball has lost its shape." Against England that same year, Boycott had trouble against the Indian spinners, playing only the first Test. During the second innings, a cheeky Solkar threatened to run him out. A livid Boycott grouched, "Don't laugh boy, I will make you crawl." Solkar's response was a stoic; "I will wait for that day." On the 1974 tour of England, in the game against Yorkshire at Bradford, Solkar came face to face with Boycs. Ashok Mankad placed a bet with Solkar that if he beat Boycs, he would buy him a pint. Ashok Mankad thought very highly of Boycott, in fact he idolised him. The wager placed, the contest was on. When Solkar managed to beat Boycott, Mankad upped the ante saying that Solkar should now get him out. Solkar bowled an armer and got Boycott leg before with Charlie Elliot ruling in his favour. Solkar was exultant, but the battle had only just begun.

In the following game against the MCC, Boycott couldn't read Solkar and was groping wondering whether the ball would come in or go out. Solkar won that day getting Boycs caught by Gavaskar. Boycott's misery continued when in the first Test at Old Trafford, he was leg before for 10 to Abid Ali. In the second innings, Solkar hovering at forward short leg stopped a glance from Boycott and threatened to run him out warning him—get back into the crease. Boycott so shaken was caught behind in the next over off Solkar for six. That gave birth to the legend—Boycott is my bunny! In fact, Boycott stopped playing Test cricket, taking a sabbatical for a while. Conditioned on the *maidans* of Bombay, Solkar knew all about sledging. Solkar reckons that this attitude amongst Mumbai players comes from over a 100-year history. He says, "It also comes from the city's lifeforce. But this attitude wasn't reserved for international cricket. It was the same when we played for Mafatlal against Tatas where the opposition would try and disturb my concentration by teasing me. It didn't bother me one bit." Another time, during a Ranji game against Maharashtra at Nasik on matting, Solkar had fever and was contemplating pulling out on the eve of the match. Ashok Mankad told Solkar to forget the fever and play. Pandurang Salgaonkar and Anwar Sheikh were bowling and the former was bowling quick. This is the same match, in which

Salgaonkar injured Sunny Gavaskar in 1974-75. Bombay was reduced to 70 for 5 when Solkar and Karsan Ghavri joined hands. Madhu Gupte was Maharashtra captain and his tail was up. Salgaonkar was bowling and in course of the over, Solkar went down the wicket and patted the matting wicket. Salgaonkar who had already scalped four victims told Solkar—I will send you back to the pavilion like I sent Gavaskar back. Solkar, ever talkative and not one to back off said—I have played John Snow, John Price and Andy Roberts, who are you? Well, Salgaonkar kept bouncing and Solkar kept smashing him. Hooking from under his chin, Solkar scored 135 while Ghavri hit 75. By making Salgaonkar bowl to his strength, not only did Solkar take the initiative away from Maharashtra, but he also upset the bowler's rhythm completely, winning the psychological battle. Gavaskar adds that only time he really raised the bar mentally was when he played against Maharashtra, "There was a real needle in those matches and I would always try and do better."

Solkar was as gritty as they came. A simple man, who came from the lower strata of society, he in many ways typifies what Bombay cricket stands for. Guts and glory. The Jamsaheb of Nawanagar sent Solkar to England and recommended him to play for Sussex second XI. Solkar says, "Tiger Pataudi saw me playing there and promoted me to the first XI. This experience stood me in very good stead when I played in England later." For instance, when Solkar batted amidst the ruins that the Indian innings was at Lord's in 1974, scoring 18 not out of 42, even hooking Chris Old for a six, it was the hours spent in the middle in

English county cricket that helped. In fact, he remembers Sir Len Hutton congratulating him after that cameo of 18 not out. That same fateful day, Solkar remembers how Amitabh Bachchan was standing at the Lord's entrance waiting for his pass. Solkar went out to meet somebody and seeing Bachchan there escorted him to the dressing room. But, that day was a disaster for Indian cricket as Arnold and Old wreaked havoc in overcast conditions.

If Vinoobhai played an important part in moulding the careers of talented youth, Vijay Merchant was equally influential, though at a different level. When he took over as chairman of the selection committee, his maxim was 'catch them young and grow them young.' Merchant who was a patron of Hindu Gymkhana also discovered Solkar. When Solkar toured Sri Lanka with the Indian schoolboys in 1963-64, it was Vijaybhai's Thackersay group, which sponsored his cricket gear. Solkar says, "Vijaybhai used to look after me and he spotted me as a potential India candidate. But Vinoobhai was the man who taught me everything. When I first shook hands with the Queen at Lord's in 1971, it was a culmination of a dream. Not only had I seen Queen Elizabeth drive down Marine Drive during her visit to Bombay, but I had seen a picture of Vinoo Mankad being introduced to her at Lord's. My dream was to shake hands with the same Queen."

While all this was happening, Bombay under the stewardship of 24-year-old Sudhir Naik won the Ranji Trophy. Naik was the only surviving batsman, for Gavaskar, Mankad, Wadekar, Sardesai and Solkar were touring. New players from that famed assembly line were initiated—

Mahesh Sampat, Ramnath Parkar and Vijay Bhosale. The onus was on Bombay to beard the lion in his own den. Bengal was the finalist, the match was at the Eden Gardens and Bombay won outright. Incidentally, Sudhir Naik never captained Bombay again because all the heavy-weights returned thereafter.

Vinoobhai's son Ashok took to the game early and was a prolific scorer for Fellowship (his school) in the Harris Shield. In 1962-63, Mankad scored 348 against Holy Name and 325 not out against Anjuman-e-Islam. In fact, he produced four successive centuries that year. His was a hard act to follow, for Vinoobhai was a colossus, a man whose deeds were legendary. Nevertheless, he sallied forth and was coached by his father at the Tairsee nets where so many of Bombay's players learnt their craft. Mankad says, "Vinoobhai was self made and so very confident of himself. His style of coaching was radically different. Once in my presence he told Paddy Shivalkar that he could be a facilitator, a bridge, but the crossing will have to be undertaken by the ward himself." Mankad believes that Vinoobhai had the eye of an eagle, for he could see the potential, nurture it and let the boy develop his own style. Vinoobhai never interfered with a person's technique. Vasant Amladi was another famous coach those days in Bombay, but he mixed theory with potential, while Vinoobhai would merely encourage and offer tips, which would take a cricketer to the next level of competency. Not only did many a Bombay players of the future like Umesh Kulkarni, Milind Rege, Sharad Hazare, Ashok Mankad,

Eknath Solkar come to the Tairsee nets, but players like Hanumant Singh and Salim Durrani would also drop in regularly and seek Vinoobhai's advice. Mankad remembers that Vinoobhai would never wake him up for practice, which was at Hindu Gym. Ashok had to get up himself and turn up on time for the nets or face his father's wrath.

Mankad reckons that Vinoobhai was a master tactician as well, for his comprehension of the nuances of the game was tremendous. He had insight. As he says, "I would discuss captaincy and match situations with Vinoobhai and use his visualisation skills to see how the game would progress. More often than not, he was bang on target." Vinoo Mankad was the first of the semi-professionals in Indian cricket. With princely states patronising cricketers and looking after their needs, cricketers like Mankad went out into the real world in search of fame and fortune. Playing in the English league or for other states where they were offered retainers, Mankad fashioned a new breed of Indian cricketers. From an aesthetic based sport, cricket slowly evolved into a need-based sport and now Mankad thinks it has become a greed-based sport. As Mankad says, "For cricketers like Vinoobhai, Vijay Manjrekar and Subhash Gupte, cricket was a means not just to earn a livelihood, but for pure survival. Cricket would keep these gents away for home for over six months of the year." Vinoobhai for example traveled to England every year between 1946 and 1959. At home, he would play for Rajasthan.

If school cricket was a stepping stone, then college and university cricket was another important phase in

Mankad's life. The Bombay University team, which boasted of Kishore Rao, Sudhir Naik and Ashok Mankad, won the Cooch Behar trophy for four successive years between 1963 and 1967. Like Sardesai, when Mankad broke into the Bombay side, he had to bat at number eight. Mankad recalls the 1970-71 twin tours. He feels that this was the golden period for the three youngsters—Sunil, Eknath and he gelled well. Mankad is unique in that even today he has scored more runs in Ranji Trophy than any other batsman. About his captaincy, Mankad says that he was always a stopgap appointment. He says, "I led when Sunil wasn't available." Remarkably three Mankads—Ashok, Atul and Rahul—followed their father into the game just as three Amarnaths followed their father in the north.

David Frith writing in *The Slow Men* says that, "Mankad raced through an over, a few quick steps and a brisk spin of a low left arm. His coach Bert Wensley from Sussex, had talked him out of wrist spin when he was young." But son Ashok refutes this. He says the Jamsaheb brought Wensley from England and he turned Vinoobhai into a spinner. Apparently, till then Vinoobhai used to bowl medium pace. Vinoo Mankad triggered off a great tradition in left arm spin bowling in Bombay. His forerunners had been Palwankar Baloo and R.J. Jamshedji, but Bapu Nadkarni, Paddy Shivalkar and Ravi Shastri followed Mankad. Padmakar Shivalkar, another man like Solkar who rose from humble beginnings, did not play Test cricket, but he was a journeyman who like many of his ilk began by playing tennis ball cricket in the lanes of Shivaji Park. After his SSC, Paddy began to look for a job but could not make any headway for three years, till Dattu Shatelkar from Bradbury Mills approached him after hearing of his cricketing skills. Dattu asked Paddy to come to Hindu Gymkhana and Bradbury Mills stalwart Subhash Gupte lent him his whites. When an apprehensive Shivalkar reached Hindu Gym with butterflies in his stomach, he saw a man in a cane chair with a season ball in his hand.

It was 1957 and the man in the cane chair tossed the ball to Shivalkar saying—I hear you can bowl, show me! Shivalkar with great trepidation asked Dattu—who is this gentleman? As Shivalkar says, "When I found out it was Vinoo Mankad, I was shivering. I went to the nets, but I couldn't focus, such was the shock." Shivalkar's first ball was in the right of the net, the second in the left corner, the season ball feeling awkward in his palm. Vinoobhai was furious and he shouted, replete with expletives—bowl at the stumps. Next, Vinoobhai asked him whether he would work for Bradbury Mills. Shivalkar's joy knew no bounds. When Shivalkar started turning out for SPG, Vinoobhai would inquire about him. He would always tell him—don't copy me; learn to bowl your own style. Shivalkar now says, "I don't know what Vinoobhai saw in me, but he guided me and I am grateful for that." Shivalkar was the philosophical spinner, wheeling away endlessly in an era where first Bapu Nadkarni and then Bishen Singh Bedi dominated. Yet, unconcerned, he would bowl without the ultimate reward, for he believed God had chosen him to bowl. He says, "I was a different person while I was bowling, I was in a trance, it was almost as if I had hypnotised myself. Around the same time, there was

Ramachandran, a very good bowler playing in Bombay cricket, but for want of opportunities, he opted for the Railways." Shivalkar feels that he was a mixture of Bapuji and Vinoobhai and he would always try and lure the batsman to his doom. He is philosophical about the fact that he couldn't play for India, like a true Hindu, he likens it to bad karma. He says, "It is destiny. There were other Bombay players like Sharad Diwadkar and Sudhakar Adhikari who too never got an opportunity. They were damn good cricketers. I once saw Jimmy Diwadkar beat and bowl Raman Subba Row at the CCI, it was a magical delivery."

Paddy Shivalkar will tell you that when he trundled into bowl, he had Vinoobhai's image in front of his eyes. Such was the man's influence on Paddy's cricket. Shivalkar's never-say-die spirit gave him innumerable wickets, but no Test cap. But he fought to the end of his illustrious career, spinning a web and making the batsman walk the gangplank of doom. Resilient and Gandhian, like the Mahatma's 'chakra', spinning away in a world of his own.

5 | When 'Maidaners' Replaced Princes

THE INSCRIPTION ON SHIVAJI MAHARAJ'S STATUE THAT imperiously looks down on the *maidan* on the western side of Dadar states that Shivaji Park was thrown open to the public in 1927 to commemorate the tercentenary of the Maratha ruler. Just as Calcutta has its *maidans* where football has become the rage, with the fabled Goshto Pal statue overlooking it, in front of the concrete superstructure called Eden Gardens, Bombay has Shivaji Park. Incubated on this *maidan* were the first commoners in Indian cricket. Two men—Vijay Manjrekar and Subhash Gupte—one a terrific batsman, the other a supreme leg spin bowler, launched their assault on the game from these humble moorings. Vijay's father Laxman Manjrekar and India's wicketkeeper on the 1936 and 1946 tours of England

D.D. Hindlekar were the best of friends. Laxman was an average cricketer, turning out for New Hind on the eastern side of Dadar (Matunga maidan) along with Ramakant Achrekar's father V.B. Achrekar. Bhandaris by caste, Manjrekar and Hindlekar Senior played in the inter-Bhandari tournament.

Vijay Manjrekar was born a batsman and he first showed signs of his talent at King George where he played alongside Hemant 'Vidhu' Hadkar. Hadkar remembers how Vijay Manjrekar from a young age had a fine technique. He was also a very good cover point fielder and was blessed with excellent strokes, particularly the hook. Hadkar and Manjrekar played together for Bombay schools. Hadkar played for Matunga Gymkhana and Bombay University later on and Vijay Manjrekar even recommended him for Rajasthan, a state which Vijay Manjrekar and Subhash Gupte both played for as professionals. Manjrekar was on the payroll of the Maharana of Mewar who played alongside him for the state. In his early years in Bombay, as Manjrekar's fame grew far and wide, another important paradigm shift was taking place in Bombay's cricket. From a predominantly south Bombay sport which had been controlled by the upper class Parsis and Gujaratis, cricket was now moving rapidly towards the lower middle class Maharashtrian stronghold of Dadar. While the *maidans*—Cross, Azad and Oval—continued to see cricket being played and the Presidency and Pentangular battles took place on the Marine Drive Gymkhanas, the seat of cricketing power remained CCI and Bombay Gymkhana, the talent pools were now northern skewed. Two prominent players who used to reside in Dadar, but for want of opportunities, played in south Bombay were P. Baloo and P.J. Churi.

The era of Parsis who had curried favour with the British by supplying labour in the docks seemed to be coming to an end, their clubs Sassanian and Elphinstone near Azad maidan burnt less brightly. Oval maidan, which divided old and new architecture, with the imposing Rajabhai Tower of Bombay University overlooking it, was a preserve of the British. Used not just for cricket, but golf and horse riding. Maharashtrians from Girgaum on their way back home from office would gather in droves and watch these activities, in the main cricket, with great interest.

Then came the Second World War, when the army requisitioned the four Gymkhanas along the Queen's necklace (Marine Drive). As the threat percept of the Japanese army grew in the east, the Gymkhanas began to be used as army barracks. Madhav Mantri adds that the war years were the coming of age of Indian and Bombay batsmanship for between 1939-46, Vijay Merchant, Vijay Hazare, Russi Modi and Russi Cooper were at the height of their powers. Mantri says that in 1942, there was a huge bomb scare in Bombay. Immediately after the attack on Pearl Harbour in December, 1941, rumour mills were agog that the Japanese would try and cripple the British Navy in Bombay Harbour to make it a twin strike. This is when decongestion began to take place in south Bombay. Families began to move from the overcongested south to north. The shifting population came to reside in Dadar. Ghettos began to sprout—Hindu Colony, Parsi Colony, South Indians in

Matunga. The proximity of the *maidan* on both the eastern and western sides, the fact that it was a railway hub and educational institutions mushrooming in the same area gave Dadar a unique representation and colour. Cricket was bound to flourish against this backdrop.

Out of these lanes and *gullies* came Vijay Manjrekar and Subhash Gupte. Subhash Gupte's brother Baloo who also played for India and served Bombay for many years in the Ranji Trophy remembers his brother's rise. Now residing in Trinidad, Subhash Gupte was named Fergie after the West Indian leg spinner W.S. Ferguson who travelled to India with Gerry Alexander in 1948. Bombay players led by Polly Umrigar gave Subhash the nickname Fergie. Baloo says that Subhash and Vijay Manjrekar were the best of friends who started their careers more or less at the same time. They first played for Mahim Juveniles and then joined Shivaji Park Gymkhana. Baloo himself joined SPG in 1952, by which time both Subhash and Manjrekar had made their debuts for India. Strangely, they played together against Nigel Howard's side in Calcutta on the eve of the New Year in December, 1951-52. This was a significant happening, for they were commoners and were erasing the last vestiges of princely hold in Indian cricket. *Maidaners* who were at the forefront of the change in Indian cricket. The transition from princes who ruled the roost in Indian cricket to the plebians was smooth. As was the transition from south Bombay to Dadar. In both cases, the contribution of Manjrekar and Gupte cannot be undermined. After all the princes had not only controlled the game directly, but also had employed young men and trained them in the art of cricket. Vinoo

Mankad and Vijay Hazare were the most prominent of such cricketers who owed everything to either the Jamsaheb of Nawanagar or the Maharaja of Baroda. The dying embers were quickly doused as the new breed of Marathi commoners made rapid strides. Subhash Gupte replaced Sadu Shinde, another leg spinner who took 6-91 against England in the first Test.

Gupte's debut was nothing to write home about, as he failed to take a wicket, while Manjrekar hit 48. Shinde came back into the side for the fourth Test. Shinde's daughter is married to politician Sharad Pawar (a former chief minister of Maharashtra), who is now the President of the MCA.

Baloo Gupte never played cricket in school, but he did play tennis ball cricket with gay abandon. During the rains, Baloo, Subhash, Manohar Hardikar and Vijay Manjrekar played in the *gullies* and on the *maidan*. Manjrekar was always the leader of the pack. Baloo began to pick up the intricacies of leg spin bowling from his brother. They would discuss the art endlessly and Subhash would bowl leg breaks at home as well. After his matriculation, Baloo joined Elphinstone, while Madhav Apte and Subhash shifted to Ruia. Baloo found in Vinoo Mankad and Madhav Mantri two excellent coaches at Elphinstone. They would make Baloo Gupte bowl alone in special nets and then make him bowl against right and left handed batsmen in another net. Baloo remembers how Mantri used to push him to the very edge of the precipice, making him bowl leg breaks till he would get the length right. While Subhash and Manjrekar turned professionals and began to ply their trade for Bengal and Rajasthan, Baloo took up a job with SBI and settled down in Bombay. Between Bapu Nadkarni, Sharad Diwadkar and Baloo Gupte, Bombay had a perfect spin attack.

Baloo Gupte, like his brother, practised long and hard. Returning from school, he would bowl at Madhu Patil in the Shivaji park nets. Since it was a difficult art, it gave him much gratification to beat the bat even in the nets with a leg break. The competition was stiff, for Maharashtra had Chandu Borde, while Tamil Nadu had V.V. Kumar bowling leg break. Subhash Gupte was shorter than his brother and more of a conventional leg spinner with a straighter one and an excellent googly. Baloo was more like Sadhu Shinde, bowling fastish leg breaks. When Baloo was a schoolboy, Subhash spent a lot of time with him, but once he became a professional, he would go to England to play league cricket. He did this continuously for eight years. As Baloo got better, he concentrated on the straighter one and leg breaks, occasionally slipping in the googly. Amazingly, Baloo Gupte grew up to replace his own brother in the Indian side. Subhash Gupte was dropped for the fourth Test at Madras and Baloo Gupte made his debut in the 1960-61 series against Fazal Mahmood's Pakistan. Like Subhash on his debut, Baloo failed to get a wicket. Baloo was dropped for the next Test, as Vaman Kumar made his debut taking 5-64 and 2-68. Subhash Gupte was an icon to the younger generation in and around Shivaji Park. Similarly, he was a folk hero in the Caribbean where he ultimately settled down. Baloo Gupte played three Tests for India taking three wickets, while S.G. Shinde played seven Tests taking 12 wickets.

But Baloo Gupte had his place in the sun, particularly the sublime spell in a Duleep Trophy final against South when in a matter of 15 overs, he claimed nine wickets including Jaisimha's and Abbas Ali Baig's. That day, the leg break worked like a charm, as Polly Umrigar caught three batsmen out in the slips in Calcutta on what was a good batting wicket. Jaisimha, before he died, told me about another incident involving Baloo Gupte. Jaisimha, always talkative and anecdotal, summarised why Bombay was always a superior side those days. He said, "Bombay was wired to win, Hyderabad was a good side bristling with big names, but it never developed the habit of winning. I feel had we won even once, we would have never looked back. But that is like saying if wishes were horses...." Jaisimha said, "In the 1964-65 final at Hyderabad, we blew it. Baloo Gupte had me caught at mid off and as I walked, he exulted—*jeet gaye match*. Such was their confidence." Jaisimha remembered the Hyderabad line up on paper— Jayantilal, Abbas Ali Baig, Tiger Pataudi, Jai, Abid Ali, Govindraj, Krishnamurthy and Mumtaz Husain and yet no Ranji Trophy title in the sixties and seventies.

Subhash Gupte went from strength to strength. Diminutive, only five feet four inches tall, he had a brisk six yard run and a vicious wrist action which gave him prodigious turn. Gupte made his name against the West Indies in the 1952-53 series where he was soon to be revered by those of Indian descent. Bowling against the West Indian juggernaut led by Frank Worrell, Everton Weekes and Clyde Walcott, Gupte was unafraid of being hit. Big-hearted and constantly attempting something different, Gupte was the toast of the Caribbean, bowling marathon spells and picking up wickets. In harness with a much senior Vinoo Mankad and later against Pakistan, forming a troika along with Ghulam Ahmed, Gupte was in his elements. This was the first edition of the trinity of Brahma-Vishnu-Maheshwar which would serve Indian cricket in the spin department. This was also the first golden age of Indian spin. Although he was the youngest of the three, he was the most attacking. Trevor Bailey writing about Gupte: "His style was classical and his method ageless. I only batted against him once in a rain affected game at Ilford, when he took two wickets, including mine on a pitch more suited to seam rather than spin." Bailey goes on to say that unlike many spinners, Fergie never suffered from sore fingers, because his break was essentially the product of a superbly supple and subtle wrist. It also explained why his googly was so hard to pick. His control was exceptional, especially for a bowler who had the ability to achieve turn on plumb pitches and he was never content to be mechanical. He was forever varying his pace and trajectory, which was one of the reasons why a lot of batsmen found it difficult to pick the Gupte wrong-un.

If Wadekar was inspired by Manjrekar, then Vengsarkar loved Wadekar's batting. Wadekar says that no Bombay cricketer of the 1960s who managed to play at the highest level can deny the debt they owe Vijay Manjrekar for his guidance and encouragement. In fact, he was quick to spot flaws in the technique of some of the younger players. Just prior to India's departure to the West Indies in 1970-71, it was Manjrekar who supervised the nets. Dilip Sardesai was one of the men in the nets and many believe that he resembled Manjrekar most in style and gait. A compulsive hooker, Manjrekar drove and cut with equal aplomb. On England's tour of India in 1961-62, Manjrekar scored 583 in a series, which India won 2-0. Stories abound about Manjrekar's introverted character and his stylistic batting. Ted Dexter who led England in that series wrote, "I have never appreciated the extent to which a batsman could be in total control, and I mean total control of what he is doing and of everything the bowler was trying to do with him."

Old timers still recall that Gupte's control was immaculate and it was very difficult to pull him through mid-wicket. Mantri who played with both says that these two were the first real models for Maharashtrian boys who aspired to emulate them. Ramakant Desai was another who was popular with the children.

Hadkar says that Manjrekar used to play with 'khunnas' against Dadar Union, while turning out for Shivaji Park. Practically every big match found Manjrekar scoring against the old enemy. When Gupte, his chum, played for DU, Manjrekar's battle with him was a feast for the connoisseurs. Playing for Rajasthan against Mysore (now Karnataka), Manjrekar was locked in a duel with B.S. Chandrasekhar, when Chandra slipped in his quick 'Bosie.' Chandra thought he had his man, but what he didn't see was Manjrekar at the very last second deftly chopping it to third man for four. Always imperious and a touch arrogant, Manjrekar ran up to the non-striker's end and patted Chandra's behind with his bat, acknowledging—good ball, but not good enough for Vijay Manjrekar.

Sujit Mukherji writing about Manjrekar is almost lyrical in his praise, "Stroke by stroke he remains India's most attractive batsman today, but has fallen short of that unutilitarian artistry which would have surely related him to popping crease potentates. He too has been tempered by the spirit of the time and emerged a highly competent craftsman, but not a creative artist: an exemplary type, not an inimitable individual. With strong invisible wrist work, rather than with muscular force he speeds away the ball as well as imparts chosen direction." Manjrekar, it is said, never did true justice to his outstanding talent, but yet he is remembered as one of India's greatest batsmen and undoubtedly the progenitor of the Maharashtrian brigade. The man who unleashed the masses, even as the classes abdicated their reign on the monarchy. Sardesai who revered both Manjrekar and Gupte thinks that the former could have scored many more runs, but for problems with application and the fact that he played in an era when selectors were always waiting with long knives to teach cricketers a lesson or two. Sardesai says, "I have seen Manjrekar hook Hall and Gilchrist keeping the ball down, it was thrilling stuff. Manjrekar would always tell me never play back to an off spinner and he himself got out to Fred Titmus playing exactly like that. He was a wonderful batsman just as Gupte was the greatest spinner in my book." Though it must be mentioned that Neil Harvey played Gupte marvelously well, besting him with some attacking strokeplay.

Both Gupte and Manjrekar first played together for Mahim Juveniles, which was a stone's throw away from

Shivaji Park. That was the time that SPG had a team of elderly people. On Diwali day those days, there was an annual fixture, a two-day festival match between Mahim Juveniles and SPG. When the younger elements began to band together, a team called Red XI was formed which saw the likes of Subhash Gupte, Manjrekar and Ramu Adhikari among others leading the way. A lot of cricket was played in the Shivaji Park area. In these tournaments, Red XI thrashed everybody and with people like N J Mhatre and Patwa taking the lead, the Red XI was turned into Shivaji Park Gymkhana 'A' team. Gradually, these players began to represent the frontline SPG outfit and it was only a matter of time before the considerable talent of Manjrekar and Gupte began to dwarf the national and international stage. The people who followed him—Sunil Gavaskar, Dilip Vengsarkar and Sachin Tendulkar, did what Manjrekar could not achieve fully in terms of statistics.

Along with Manjrekar and Gupte, there was a third Bombay player who emerged almost at the same time. The era of Merchant, Modi and Hazare was coming to an end. Against the West Indies in 1948-49, Pahlon Ratanji Umrigar made his debut at the Kotla in the second Test. Though dropped for the rest of the series, Polly Umrigar was in many ways India's lucky mascot, playing a part in India's first eight Test victories. The first thing that strikes you about Polly kaka, as Bombay likes to call him, are his huge hands. These hands made him a very safe catcher. Polly kaka resurfaced in the same series that saw Manjrekar and Gupte make their debuts, against Nigel Howard's inexperienced English side. The first four Tests saw nothing of note from him till he was included in the side for the fifth Test at the last moment. India one Test behind were looking to level the series, more importantly, they were looking for that elusive first Test victory. Polly Umrigar batting at number seven hit 130 not out to contribute to that win as India won by an innings and eight runs.

Polly Umrigar's tryst with the game was also fortuitous. It was as a 12-year-old in Sholapur that he found himself pitchforked into a game where one side was a man short. As a footballer and hockey player, Umrigar had good ball sense. So, he took very well to fielding. Now a sprightly 75, Polly kaka remembers that first game as clear as daylight, saying that he stood at deep fine leg. A certain Mr Pandey roped in all the Parsi boys in Sholapur and put together a team. Jehangir Nagarvala was the side's coach and he taught young Umrigar to get behind the ball and play in line. When Umrigar's father was transferred back to Bombay, Umrigar began to play Kanga League for Lord Northbrooke Club (a Parsi club). From Bharda H.S., Umrigar went to St. Xavier's college and finally played for Young Zoroastrians. Soon, he broke into the Bombay team as a bowler in 1946. And it was team of titans—Russi Modi, K.C. Ibrahim, Russi Cooper, Vijay Merchant, Madhav Mantri and Dattu Phadkar. Polly Umrigar grew in an atmosphere that could only be described as conducive to the development and flowering of young talent. Umrigar says, "While playing the Pentangular for Parsis against the Hindus, I remember Vijaybhai coming to me after the game and telling me that I should play a particular shot in a particular manner. There were inspirational figures all around—Madhav Mantri and Vinoo Mankad would always have a word or two for youngsters like me."

Though the 1952 tour of England was nothing short of an unmitigated disaster for Umrigar as Trueman and Alec Bedser made sure that he didn't cross 15 in a single innings, Umrigar bounced back against the Pakistanis. It was in the West Indies that he earned the sobriquet of 'palm tree hitter' as he scored 560 runs. While Umrigar enjoyed that tour immensely, he has fonder memories of the Black Bradman, George Headley, coming to the Combined Universities dressing room on their 1948-49 tour of India and telling Umrigar—well played, young man—after Umrigar hit an unbeaten 130. This inspired Umrigar to greater heights. On the 1952-53 tour of the West Indies, Madhav Apte (also from Bombay), Subhash Gupte, Manjrekar were in the frontline. All four of them performed creditably. Umrigar and Manjrekar had replaced the stalwarts and the race to score runs was on between the two of them. If one goes back in the Wellsian Time Machine, one will find that Umrigar and Manjrekar competed with one another to score more runs. Normally batting at numbers three and four in the Indian batting order, the Umrigar-Manjrekar battle proved beneficial for India as both scored over 3000 runs in Test cricket. Manjrekar actually ended his Test career with a hundred against New Zealand in 1964-65, something that Gavaskar failed to do, out for 96 at Bangalore against Pakistan in 1986-87.

Umrigar captained Bombay to the Ranji title thrice. He says, "We used to rely on our batting. Moreover our strength, determination and will to win was what ensured that we kept winning. Our strong point was our batting, we knew that we could outscore the opposition and this was what our rivals feared." Umrigar thinks that Bombay's cricketing ethos is similar to Punjab's in hockey. He says, "Sometimes, growth as a product of a particular culture takes place in a certain centre. So, it was with cricket and Bombay. The opposition was normally very apprehensive of the hiding that our batsmen would give them." All that is now in the past, for cricket has spread far and wide in India now. But men like Umrigar and Vinoo Mankad will be remembered for long. Even today as one enters the Wankhede stadium in Mumbai, the gates have been named after these legendary sportsmen.

6 | Cricket's Haridwar

LIKE THE HINDU LOTUS FLOWER EMERGING FROM A murky pond, the beauty and grandeur of Indian cricket blooms from the rough and shabby earthiness of the Matunga maidan. It may appear undignified, especially when compared to the manicured lawns of the Cricket Club of India or Bombay Gymkhana, yet no institution is nurtured with so much attention and love. Nowhere more than the *maidans* of Bombay is such a cross-section of urban society better represented; displaying diversity of wealth, caste, profession, ability and age—Emma Levine writing evocatively in *A Kind of Pilgramage*.

If England had Yorkshire, Bombay had Dadar, the western and eastern sides of this enclave producing cricketers mechanically. If Vijay Manjrekar and Subhash Gupte heralded the emergence of the Maharashtrian superstars, then Polly Umrigar played his part towards reviving the Parsis. Nari Contractor, Russi Surti, Farokh Engineer followed Umrigar and played for India. All three deserted Bombay, the first two for Gujarat for want of more opportunities in their home state while the stylish Engineer played for Bombay and then decided to become a county professional with Lancashire. The game was alive and well in the very heart of Bombay. The balance of power had shifted out of south Bombay. If Kent for instance produced three of the greatest glovemen the game has seen in Leslie Ames, Godfrey Evans and Allan Knott, then Dadar turned out four of the best that India has seen—Hindlekar, Madhav Mantri, Naren Tamhane and Farokh Engineer. There was also Chandu Patankar and Ramakant Achrekar who played in the same area.

Mantri says that in an era in which clubs were developed on communal lines (this was the case with the Gymkhanas on Marine Drive) Dadar Union shone like a beacon, for it was the first truly cosmopolitan club. Started by a splinter faction of New Hind led by Minoo Lawyer, Deshmukh and Luma Kenny in 1927, it became a hub around which other clubs mushroomed. The cult of cricket was common. On the eastern side of Dadar, facing the Matunga maidan, as many as five clubs thrived—Dadar Union, Matunga Gymkhana, New Hind Sporting Club, Dadar Parsi Zoroastrians and Dadar Parsi Colony. Matunga maidan was rechristened Major Ramesh Dadkar Kreedangan in the memory of Dadkar who perished in the 1971 operations. Mantri and Polly Umrigar say that the Parsis, though a minority really kickstarted the game in the city. Mantri says that such was

H.D. Kanga's attachment to the game that when he was sick, Vijay Merchant would pay him regular visits to keep him abreast with the happenings in local cricket.

That was a different era and a different time zone. In front of Ruia College, on the Matunga maidan—Madhav Mantri, Vasant and Mohini Amladi, T.B. Vinod, S.M. Shankar, Madhav Iyer, Vasu Paranjpe, Naren Tamhane—would gather and practise in the month of May. Dadar Union team members would practice fielding. People like Subhash Gupte and Arun Wardhe who played for Dadar Union, then played for Shivaji Park Gymkhana. It is said that Dadar Union's 12th man was P.K. 'Joe' Kamath (who later became Bombay coach) and he was being enticed by Goud Saraswats to play for them. Such was Kamath's commitment that he opted to remain 12th man for DU. Mantri joined the club in 1940 and over the years he saw the rise of Manjrekar and Gupte on the western side. Followed by Ramakant Desai, these were the first superstars amongst Maharashtrians on the Shivaji Park side.

Inter-collegiate cricket was simultaneously a big drawcard. Teams like Elphinstone, St Xavier's, Ruia, Siddarth and to a lesser extent Sydenham were fighting for honours. Boys like Naren Tamhane, rated by many as India's best wicket keeper ever, came through this mill. Tamhane says that the ethos in Hindu Colony, Dadar was incredible. He says, "We were all products of *gully* cricket. Matches were played between the first six lanes. From here as we got better, we graduated to playing in front of Ruia College." Tamhane took the gloves from Mantri in Dadar Union in an era where discipline was stringently enforced and great importance given to out-cricket like fielding and running between the wickets. Tamhane like many Bombay players of the past profited from spending time in the middle (in local cricket) with legends like Merchant. Tamhane particularly remembers the time Merchant flogged the DU attack for 280 in a Purshottam Shield game.

Tamhane used local, domestic and international cricket to move up the value chain as it were. He tried to copy Mantri as a youngster and then spoke to West Indian Gerry Alexander and Bill Langley of England about skills required for wicket keeping. This was also the time that members of the CKP (Chandrasenia Kayastha Prabhu) caste residing in Dadar took to the game very aggressively. A former club cricketer says, "Everybody knew everyone else in Hindu Colony. After a match as we would get down from the local and walk down the bridge, people in their balconies would either applaud one or show their displeasure." There was an element of oneness.

It was essentially the central and western railway bridges, which differentiated between Shivaji Park and Hindu Colony. With CKPs at the vanguard, the historical and sociological background needs to be examined. History tells us that Baji Prabhu Deshpande, a CKP warrior in the Maratha army defended Shivaji Maharaj when the Mughals in Vishalgarh encircled him. Deshpande defended Shivaji Maharaj's rear when he escaped from Pawankhind. In the process Deshpande lost an arm and his deed of valour has been recorded for posterity. This tale was famous amongst middle class Maharashtrians those days. While Madhav Mantri, Sunil Gavaskar, Vengsarkar, Tendulkar, Milind

Rege are Goud Saraswats, many of the cricketers those days were CKPs.

Amongst Maharashtrian Brahmins, there are two sects, Deshast (those from the mainland) and Konkanst (those residing on the coast). CKPs and GSBs (Goud Saraswat Brahmins) are the dominant castes within these Brahmins. Folklore tells us that during Rana Pratap's time, two different segments of Rajputs came to reside in Maharashtra (Marathas) and Nepal (Ranas). CKPs, however, seen as 'sena of the chandrama' or army of the moon, are the community which really took to cricket. Never short of valour on the cricket field, they have bolstered Bombay's cricket over the years, along with the Goud Saraswats. Many sociologists reckon that this immaculate work ethic that Bombay's cricketers have displayed comes from the zeal that their caste brings to bear.

Sunil Gavaskar for instance used to have special nets at Matunga maidan where he would call up his DU team-mates like Urmikant Modi, Narayan Pai, V.S. 'Marshall' Patil and Jitu Botha to bowl at him. Dilip Vengsarkar and Ramnath Parkar who played with Gavaskar at DU would bat endlessly. Gavaskar says, "We practiced a lot against these bowlers bowling from 16-17 yards in the nets which meant that the ball would come that much quicker. We used to bat on concrete as well, so one had to watch the ball till the last moment." Gavaskar would do this whenever he had a bad patch. But even otherwise, every Saturday morning saw Vengsarkar and others bat in the nets between 7 and 11. Vengsarkar says, "This was the most serious practice of my life. I think the tightness of the game that people refer to about DU batsmen came from these long hours of practice."

Mantri who coached at Elphinstone and DU was typically old school, always a strict disciplinarian, holding the lofty values of the gentleman's game uppermost in his mind. Mantri says, "I learnt from Homi Vajifdar who played for the Parsis and Bombay. He gave great importance to fielding and bowling line and length. I used to follow Vajifdar's pattern." Both Vajifdar and Mantri had a special net for bowlers where three lines and three good length spots were earmarked. It is believed that Vajifdar was instrumental in honing Dattu Phadkar's skills as a bowler. Mantri remembers the game between Elphinstone and Maharashtra where Phadkar and Amladi bowled them out for a paltry 49. Similarly, while batting Mantri learnt from the masters of yore. Duleepsinhji who was a regular at CCI always gave tips to youngsters. Mantri says, "He would tell me, while playing a spinner try and take the ball on the full toss as much as possible and hit it, instead of making it a half volley. It is also said that Subhash Gupte never bowled in the nets to either Manjrekar or Madhav Apte, for they were butchers of leg spin bowling, twinkling footwork with rasping cuts and compact drives in front of the wicket, acting as enablers.

Vasu Paranjpe is another diehard Dadar Unionite who grew up near Matunga maidan which he describes as a 'patch of life' that had everything around it—schools, colleges, Gymkhanas and of course cricket. He feels that the Kanga league on wet wickets was the best education for batsmen, but once pitches began to be covered in 1972, it

above: Farokh Engineer, wicket-keeper and opening batsman extraordinaire played many a memorable knock for India.

left: Passing of the baton — Vijay Manjrekar with Wadekar.

below: The Manjrekars: Father, Vijay and son, Sanjay.

Abhey Kuruvilla who was Mumbai's spearhead in the nineties.

below left: Ajit Agarkar hasn't done his talent justice.

below: Amol Muzumdar couldn't break into the big league.

opp. page: Dilip Vengsarkar, strokes the ball. (right) Ravi Shastri, lifting his spirits. (below) On flight to the West Indies the Indian team catches a few winks of much needed sleep. Seen in the picture are Dilip Vengsarkar (foreground) and Ravi Shastri.

Sameer Dighe

Top: Tendulkar plays Australian Paul Wilson off his hip.

Vinod Kambli

above left : Sandip Patil signing autographs during a friendly match in Mumbai in 1999.

above right : Crowd during a cricket match in Bombay.

above : Sachin the real crowd puller.

below : Children playing cricket is serious business.

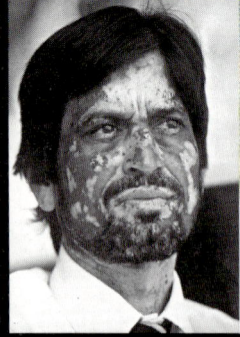

above: Captains all — Mumbai's pride — from L to R : Sharad Diwadkar, Sandeep Patil, Milind Rege, G S Ramchand, Madhav Mantri, Ajit Wadekar, Sunil Gavaskar, Raju Kulkarni, Sachin Tendulkar, Ashok Mankad, Bapu Nadkarni, Lalchand Rajput, Dilip Sardesai. Sitting (L to R) Amol Mazumdar, Sameer Dighe and Vinod Kambli with the grand prize, the Ranji Trophy.

below: Bombay team lift the Ranji Trophy in 1995.

lost a lot of its charm. As youngsters, Paranjpe and others would go and watch club cricket for it had character. If Fort Vijay had Vijay Merchant and Karsan Bhatia, then Sunder CC had Vinoo Mankad and Dattu Phadkar. Parsi Cyclists had the Irani brothers, Polly Umrigar and Nari Contractor while New Hind had Hindlekar and J.L. Patil and Jolly CC had the Apte brothers—Madhav and Arvind, Khushubhai Jobanputra, Raiji brothers and Vithalbhai Zaveri and finally CCI had G.S. Ramchand, A.B. Abraham, S.L. Patil (who was a contemporary of Vinoobhai) and Vijay Merchant. In the Matunga area, youth had different methods, but the purpose was the same—to excel in cricket. The rapport between the old and young, of course, gave the game fillip.

Between 1966 and 1992, DU was a behemoth in local cricket winning 85 per cent of all the tournaments from Comrades Shield to Talim to Purshottam to Kanga League. Paranjpe says, "Everybody knew his job and as such the team was highly motivated and focused." This kinship manifested itself in different ways. Paranjpe, a father figure to the younger players would pick up Milind Rege, Sunny Gavaskar and later Dilip Vengsarkar in his car and drive to the ground. In the car, only cricket was discussed. Such was the commitment. And Paranjpe sitting in his Hindu Colony home will proudly tell you that he doesn't remember a day when he didn't pick up the three boys and as it happened all three of them would always be ready and waiting. In a celebrated incident, Mantri once dropped Ramnath Kenny who was already a Test player because he came only 25 minutes before the start of a match. When Paranjpe's son Jatin began to play for DU, Sunny was still playing. After a game where Sunny was batting with Jatin, the maestro came to Vasu Paranjpe's home in the evening and said— now I am really getting old, first I played alongside you and now I am playing with your son.

The game was pure and undiluted in that era, is the common refrain of the stars of yesteryears. Bapu Nadkarni says by playing against legendary names that had records at the highest level, we could only learn and hope to imbibe their skills. And some of these journeymen played for years. Vasant Amladi at the age of 46 batting for Tatas versus ACC scored a fluent hundred against Ramakant Desai at his best. The innings took the breath away of all those who watched. Such incidents are a dime a dozen in Bombay cricket. Similarly in the SPG vs DU battles, Y B Patwa, who was lame and a left arm spinner would always get Ramnath Kenny's wicket. The case of Sudhakar Adhikari is probably the most galling. While Kenny and Hardikar played for India, SPG's Adhikari, who was a heavy scorer in the Ranji Trophy, never got a look in to the Indian team. Sudhakar Adhikari and Paddy Shivalkar like many others were unsung heroes who never got the opportunity at the highest level. When Sunder CC played Parsi Cyclists, Phadkar used to give Umrigar a harrowing time.

Stories abound. Like Pankaj Roy batting against Subhash Gupte in the nets at CCI, unable to pick the leg spinner's googly. Vijay Merchant watching from the sidelines called out to Roy and asked—can't you pick him, watch Gupte's wrist and see its trajectory in the air. Vijay Hazare used to actually bring the Baroda Cricket

Association side to Bombay immediately after the conclusion of the Kanga league and play for a fortnight against various clubs for match practice.

The biggest deterrent for Bombay players was that there so many of them who came at the same time because of this cricketing culture. The fortunate ones broke through, while others languished in club and domestic cricket. Others grabbed the opportunity with both hands. Merchant and Mankad, Polly Umrigar, Vijay Manjrekar, Subhash Gupte, Ramakant Desai, Ajit Wadekar, Dilip Sardesai, Sunil Gavaskar, Dilip Vengsarkar, Sachin Tendulkar are some of the names that will always burn brighter than others. On the western side of Dadar too, there was a 'patch of life,' Shivaji Park, which had its own history and tradition. The Gymkhana made famous by Manjrekar and Gupte earlier used to be known as Maharashtra- Hindu CC. It was in 1948 that it became Shivaji Park Gymkhana when the chief minister of Bombay, Morarji Desai, ensured that the communal slant in sporting clubs should be ended post haste. Jwaule who was Mayor of the city and R.K. Vaidya who was the local corporator were members of the Maharashtra-Hindu Club. The original club was started in a typing class near the railway station on the eastern side where officegoers would gather. It was on the eastern side that the British camp was ensconced and this is where cricket had first sprung up. Running parallel to the railway tracks, this area became the centre of sporting activity, just as Azad maidan had been so in South Mumbai.

As nationalism took jingoist overtones, the British wanted to divert the attention of the youth. Successive

Bombay Governors thus gave cricket the necessary impetus. The mills were also hotbed of nationalistic fervour. The battle for the youth's mind was being fought at a subterranean level. The British using cricket as a carrot, while the nationalists were propagating ethnic sport. Along Gokhale Road in Dadar (where Vijay Manjrekar later stayed), *vyayamshalas* mushroomed. Supported and covertly encouraged by nationalists like Sayaji Rao Gaekwad of Baroda, Manik Rao, Shahu Maharaj of Kolhapur and Kale Guruji, these *vyayam mandirs* where indigenous sport and ethnic martial arts were practiced were radically opposed to the British. Most importantly, the legend of Shivaji Maharaj and tales of his fabled exploits were recounted. It was a clear case of local gymnasium versus Gymkhanas. In these *vyayamshalas* an undergound movement to train boys in ethnic martial arts began to take root. But cricket and the Gymkhanas triumphed. The lower middles class inhabitants of Dadar were encouraged by the British to take up jobs and play cricket. The first signs of cricket taking a hold over the masses in this area were seen as far back as the First World War.

The Shivaji Park Gymkhana pavilion was built in 1932 and Madhusudan Patil joined it in 1934 by paying Rs 35. Down the road was Mahim Juveniles, the club which later produced Vijay Manjrekar and Subhash Gupte. This was a mill club for the lower middle class mill workers while SPG came to be known as the club for middle class officegoers. Once the pavilion was in place, and many more Maharashtrians began to move northwards from south Bombay during the Second World War, the club's popularity grew. Many believe that SPG acted as a huge catalyst for the area's growth. Madhu Patil, now a sprightly 81, remembers how the British began to break down the barriers by inviting the various clubs which had grown in the area to play against them on Saturdays. Madhu Patil's father Sridhar Manik Patil and uncle Harishchandra Manik Patil both played the game. Dhoti, one pad and one glove, in outfits which look suspiciously like those worn by the villagers of Champaner in the hit film *Lagaan*, were what these cricketers would turn out in. The style was cross-bat and intent very aggressive. Harishchandra Patil or Haribhau became the president of SPG and encouraged the youth like his nephew Madhusudan to take to the game.

Slowly the SPG team of elderly people began to give way to younger members who had by now begun to earn. It was actually during SPG's silver jubilee in 1934 that many middle class Maharashtrians became members. After independence, CCI decided to encourage two cricketers annually and thus started a scholarship programme. Among the first were two SPG boys, who had come up the ranks from Mahim Juveniles (described as tentwallahs those days as they were from the poorer strata of society). Their names: Vijay Manjrekar and Subhash Gupte, who were selected to play league cricket in England. The battles between the two neighbours—DU and SPG—were famous. Duleepsinhji once watching DU and its fielding and bowling ability remarked—this is a team playing. If Calcutta football had its Derby in the shape of Mohun Bagan playing East Bengal, this was Bombay cricket's equivalent. In the Kanga league V.S. Patil has scalped 759 wickets, which remains a record till this day. But the late Ramakant Desai is the fourth highest wicket taker with 459, while Paddy Shivalkar of SPG is the third highest with 564 wickets.

If three generations of Manjrekars and Gavaskars have played cricket, then three generation of Patils have also played. Sandeep Patil, flamboyant strokeplayer and in many ways a precursor to Sachin Tendulkar gave us only fleeting pleasure. Two of his most famous attacking innings' however were played at the highest level—174 against a marauding Dennis Lillee, Rodney Hogg and Len Pascoe at the Adelaide Oval after being felled in the previous Test at the SCG. And an unbeaten 129 against Bob Willis, Ian Botham and Derek Pringle at Old Trafford a season later in 1982. Sandeep Patil says, "It was a case of instant recall, all of us couldn't think of anything other than cricket while we were growing up." Many believe that the amount of tennis ball cricket played during the rains by Shivaji Park boys enabled them to hit the ball harder. Patil was undoubtedly a dasher like his father before him. He feels that all the schools and colleges like Balmohan Vidymandir, King George, Chabildas, Ruia, Podar and Shardashram also played a part in the proliferation of good cricketers. Sandeep says, "From the time Vijay Manjrekar became a star, everybody in Shivaji Park seemed obsessed with batting. Bowling was seen as part of a slave syndrome, *chalo kaam karo*! Everybody I knew in and around the *maidan* had some connection with cricket." If cricket is seen as a leveller, then Mumbai's *maidans* remain the best example of equality. Everybody practises his art form with great diligence and devotion, irrespective of caste or religion, poverty or wealth or level of proficiency.

Milind Rege who saw Sandeep Patil as a young man was immediately impressed with his dashing style. He says, "he was batting at number eight for SPG. I told myself, hello this boy can bat. When I watched him score 75 in a Century Rayon vs Tatas game in the mid 1970s, my hunch proved right. I took him to CCI and made him bat at number three. This upset a lot of people." The moot point here is that Sandeep Patil made such rapid strides that from Times Shield, it took him little time to vault into the Test side. Now coach of Kenya, Patil sparkled briefly scoring 1588 runs in 29 Tests, but had a much longer stint in the Ranji Trophy where he turned a lesser state like Madhya Pradesh into a fighting unit. Just as Chandrakant Pandit, another able Bombay hand, wicket keeper and batsman went to Assam and later Madhya Pradesh, Patil spread the message of cricket as a professional. M.P. finally reached the final of the Ranji Trophy in 1998-99 losing to Karnataka at Bangalore. The tide had turned by this time and new stars from new areas were coming to the fore. Debashish Mohanty and Shiv Sunder Das from Orissa, Harbhajan Singh from Punjab, Zaheer Khan from Baroda (though originally from Maharashtra), V.V.S. Laxman from Hyderabad *et al*. Now young Vinayak Mane, on whom Mumbai's hopes and aspirations are focused carries the cross to perform. Having batted sensibly against the visiting Australians, the young boy is playing for Shivaji Park Youngsters. Yes, the same team which saw Sachin Tendulkar make a mark. Will he be weighed down by the expectations of his city? Only time will tell.

7 | The Early Years

THE ENTERPRISING PARSIS LED THE WAY FOR THE development of cricket in Bombay. If the sub-continent has become the epicentre of global cricket, then some of the credit must go to the Parsis who passionately took to the game over 120 years ago. Pertinently, it was football that played an important part in Indians asserting their nationalistic aspirations on the eastern seaboard in Calcutta. As far back as 29 June, 1911 against the backdrop of Fort William, Mohun Bagan played the East Yorkshire Regiment in the Indian Football Association Shield final, barefoot Indians taking on arrogant and pugnacious Englishmen. Mohun Bagan won that game 2-1 and in many ways dented the British psyche. The Bengalis scored brownie points, but it is the Parsis who stood out with their exemplary work in cricket's propagation, supported and encouraged as they were by the ruling elite.

While it is well known that Calcutta became the seat of Indian football, cricket in India also has its origins in Job Charnock's city. As far back as 1792, the Calcutta Cricket Club was established. But the game did not flower as the 'natives' did not show great enthusiasm for it. Meanwhile, the Parsis in Bombay played to the tune of the British. With the creation of the Orient Club in 1848, the Indianisation of the game, or should one say the 'Parsisation' of the game was well on its way. The Orient gave way to Young Zoroastrians and as Polly Umrigar recounts, "The well-to-do Parsi families who were traders and had interests in shipping and consequently in the organising of contract labour took the lead and helped the formation of Parsi cricket teams in the early years." They took to the game with unbelievable gusto and zest. Touring England in 1886 and then again in 1888, the Parsis were encouraged by the British Royal family. *Cricket Chat* wrote about the tour, "Anything which can tend to promote an assimilation of tastes and habits between the English and the native-subjects of our Empress Queen cannot fail to conduce to the solidity of the British Empire. The zeal with which the natives of India are working to secure proficiency in the chief as well as the best of our sports cannot be overestimated. The Parsi fraternity is the most intelligent as well as the most loyal of the races scattered over our Indian possession." A trifle condes-cending, but very accurate and apt. More English than the English was an accusation against the Parsis those days. However, there is no denying their pioneering and pathbreaking achievements in making India a cricket power. Ramachandra Guha sums up their role most succinctly. Writing in *Wickets in the East* he says that: "The Parsis, of course, were making their fortunes in the China opium trade even as they were taking to a game which more than one economist has since referred to as the opium of the people."

In this entire din, there had to be a turning point, similar to the Mohun Bagan versus East Yorkshire Regiment game in football. And this came 21 years before that famous football game in 1889-90. Vasant Raiji (whose father was the Divan of Baroda), cricket historian and former cricketer ensconced in his sea facing flat in Mumbai's upmarket Walkeshwar area says that "between 1886 and 1891, the Parsis used to have an annual fixture with the Bombay Gymkhana and Poona Gymkhana. The victory over G.F. Vernon's team meant that their stock rose skyhigh." The first innings saw the match even-steven with Vernon's XI making 97, followed by the Parsis who managed 80. Dr Pavri, a fast bowler and like W G Grace a doctor, bowled Vernon's side out for 61 taking 7-34 and the Parsis won by four wickets. Raiji who has done extensive research on the rise of Parsi cricket says that with the epoch-making victory, Lord Harris, then Governor of Bombay felt that the time had come for the Parsis to play a combined representation of the English based in the Bombay Presidency. This was simply because the Parsis were a very strong team by then. And so in July 1892, the first Presidency match was played. But let Raiji recount what happened, "This was known as the fire engine match and the Presidency match got off to an inauspicious start. The match was abandoned and though the fire brigade which had been called to draw the rain water off the ground tried its best, the underfoot conditions weren't conducive to cricket."

Raiji says that the Parsis were the most westernised community and they were proficient in English as well. He says, "The Englishmen were looking for competition. I think it was purely incidental that by encouraging cricket played by the Parsis, they managed to further their business interests. I don't think one can attribute any motive for the growth of the game those days." The Presidency matches carried on till 1906 when the Hindus joined in, making it a triangular contest. Raiji says that between 1892 and 1906, 26 matches were played of which the Parsis won 11, the Europeans won 10 and five matches were drawn. Played in August and September in Bombay and Poona, the games were sellouts. It was Lord Harris who as Governor of Bombay allowed the three communities—Parsis, Hindus and Muslims to build Gymkhanas along the seafront.

Mihir Bose writing in *The History of Indian Cricket* says that Harris used the Parsis as a counterweight to the increasing criticism, which his insensitive rule provoked from educated Indians. He writes, "Gopal Krishna Gokhale, the great leader of Indian moderates—and the Guru of Gandhi—described Harris's rule as unsympathetic and reactionary administration." Cricket, which fulfilled the Victorian ideal of the manly game, was, for Harris, just the 'healthy, active pastime as a counter-attraction to pice (Indian for penny) and politics.' Nevertheless, cricket became a great social occasion with Lord Harris himself watching practically all the games. J.M. Framjee Patel, captain of Parsis in *Stray Thoughts on Indian Cricket* writes,

"These matches are getting more and more popular every day and what is more they are taking a stronger hold on the masses. Cricket is a prolific entertainer for the classes and the masses."

In 1907, the Hindus led by C.V. Mehta, a textile magnate, entered their team and made it a three-way battle. Palwankar Baloo was the dominant bowler in this era. The race was on and by 1912, the Muslims had joined in. Cricket was thriving. The four Palwankar brothers—P. Baloo, P. Shivram, P. Vithal and P. Ganpat, played for the Hindus in 1914 and 1915. Frank Tarrant of the Europeans was the most dreaded bowler between 1915 and 1919. C.K. Nayudu made his debut in 1916 and after blocking the first three balls from the same Tarrant, smashed the fourth over the boundary, Nayudu had arrived with the first of his many sixes. By 1921 some of the legends of English cricket were playing—C.B. Fry, Wilfred Rhodes, George Hirst, J.H. Parsons. With cricket divided on communal lines, the growth was being stifled, because there was a clear case of too much inbreeding. For instance the Parsis had the Spencer Cup which was open to Parsis only, while the Purshottam Shield was confined to Hindus. The Europeans had their Bombay Gymkhana where nobody else was permitted. Once the Gymkhana again were formed on communal lines, there was some relief. The case of P. Baloo who died recently was most curious. A left arm spinner of immense talent, he was a Harijan or scheduled caste. So, the upper class Hindu Gymkhana would not let him enter. For his innate cricketing talent, the Gymkhana finally relented and brought him into the team, but he had to sit at a separate table during lunchtime. It was only after Bombay Gym appointed him 'grounds' bowler (to bowl in the nets) that Hindu Gymkhana became more open and changed their perception about the backward castes and Baloo in particular.

The game though appeared to be getting better and better, the standard constantly improving as men like K.S. Duleepsinhji made their mark in the Quadrangular in 1928. In the Hindus versus Parsis match, Duleep, prince and cricketer extraordinaire played R.J. Jamshedji with style, elan and panache, hitherto not seen by Bombayites. With footwork, which almost seemed magical, Duleep scored 84 and 38, the highlight being a reverse sweep to counter Jamshedji's negative bowling. In 1936 Harold Larwood played unsuccessfully for the Europeans. The following year, a team called the Rest was also given representation in the tournament, thereby making it a Pentangular. The Rest mainly comprised Christians, Anglo-Indians and Jews. By now cricket was being played completely with communal connotations and this wasn't a happy state of affairs in a turbulent phase of the nation's history when the nationalist movement was gathering momentum. Raiji says, "Nowhere in the world was cricket divided on religious lines. It was an anachronism, and by this time the entire concept of a tournament like this had outlived its usefulness. With independence approaching, nationalists were looking at a united India, as caste and religion were increasingly being put on the back burner." On the political front, though the Muslim League, was pursuing its own agenda. A separate entity is what they were seeking. Pakistan is what this new nation-state was finally called and it led to unprecedented bloodletting and mass migration. Though cricket was unaffected by these political manoeuvres, sooner than later, the politics of *satyagraha* being practised by Gandhiji saw to it that cricket too came to a standstill.

By now the tournament had become a straight face off between the Hindus and Muslims, for the Parsis and Europeans were not the force they once were. The Pentangular was now being played at the CCI and 1942 saw the tournament being cancelled, following Mahatma Gandhi's clarion call of Quit India. Raiji remembers that the venerable sports writer and commentator Bobby Talyarkhan relentlessly campaigned against the abolition of the Pentangular and by the time partition came along, the resultant bad blood drove this tournament to die a natural death. Moreover, the Pentangular was affecting the proper growth of the Ranji Trophy, which was really a national tournament, to be played all over the country. The message of cricket was to be spread with the Ranji Trophy and the Pentangular's continued popularity was asphyxiating it.

The joust between the Vijays—Merchant and Hazare was warming up by 1943. Vijay Hazare played for the weaker Rest, while Merchant did so for the Hindus. Vijay was supported by his brother Vivek, while his namesake had sibling Uday to back him up. The competition between the two saw runs and more runs from their bats. In the 1943 final, the Hindus batted first. Merchant scored 250 not out, thus torpedoing Hazare's 248 in the previous game. The Hindus scored 581 for 5 declared and the Rest were bowled out for 133 with Hazare top scoring with 59. Given the follow on, the Rest was plumbing the depths at 62 for 5 when Vivek joined Vijay. Slowly, the Rest began to fight back. At close of play on the third day, Rest was 189 for 5. The next day, Vijay Hazare, batting like a man possessed savaged the Hindu bowling. The brothers added 300 for the sixth wicket, Vijay not out 266 and Vivek 21. When Vivek departed, Vijay launched an even more ferocious assault and finally was the last man out for 309 of his team's total of 387. The Rest had been vanquished but Hazare stood tall in his heroic loneliness. Such was the competitive edge those days that in the course of the innings, C.S. Nayudu continued to bowl to Hazare despite being mauled. As C.S. Nayudu told his fellow players later—the objective was to get Hazare out and not to plot his brother Vivek's downfall—I could have tried to get Vivek out, but the real prize was to get Vijay. The following year, Denis Compton and Joe Hardstaff played for the Europeans, but they were beaten by the Parsis for whom the elegant Russi Modi scored 215 not out. Russi Cooper joined Modi as the latest avatars of Parsi batsmen with style and substance. Modi was a touch player, all timing and artistry. Lala Amarnath particularly was fond of Modi's elegance. A very good runner between wickets, Modi along with Merchant and Hazare brought the crowds flocking to the CCI.

As the pressure to abolish the Pentangular grew, the importance of the Ranji Trophy, which was being seen as a true national tournament began to be taken seriously. In a celebrated article, Bobby Talyarkhan wrote, "Is there no enjoyment, no sport, no life worth living, except when words Hindu, Muslim and Parsi come into play? Are

Indians born into this world to believe that nothing, no sport, can be enjoyed unless it is communal." The last rites of the Pentangular had been completed. Communal cricket was another page in history. Edward Docker in his seminal work *History of Indian Cricket* writes, "Very notable was the unusual atmosphere of goodwill that prevailed [in the Pentangular]. The cheerful rivalry on the field seemed to infect the thousands watching. If ever India is to win communal unity, it will be on the cricket fields, and cricket fields of Bombay in particular."

Madhav Mantri who played in the Pentangular says that between 1939 and 1946, Vijay Merchant, Vijay Hazare, Russi Modi and Russi Cooper were busy thrashing bowling attacks to all parts of the field. Until then, he says, batsmen had been reckless. Now the batting flowered as a contest for big scores ensued. Mantri says, "Merchant playing for Hindu Gymkhana or Fort never gave his wicket away. Even in the nets, he would make me keep, so that he batted in simulated match conditions. And I don't remember getting too many balls in my gloves, so precise were his foot movements and delicacy of his strokeplay." The competition was captivating, according to Mantri, with batsmen applying themselves, building big innings. C.S. Nayudu and Amir Elahi were the top leg spinners of this time. The two would always be experimenting, bowling top spinners and following it up with straighter ones. Variety was the kernel of their bowling as they tried to snare the batsman to his doom.

In one of the most challenging Pentangular matches that Mantri played in, Hindus were pitted against Muslims.

K.C. Ibrahim scored a defiant hundred and when the ninth wicket fell, the Muslims still needed four runs to win. M.S. Balooch was the last man for Muslims and Chandu Sarwate was bowling. Balooch took a wild swipe as any number 10 would do in such a situation and he got an inside edge and the ball raced down to fine leg. Mantri, ran for it as if his life depended on it. Cutting the ball off, Mantri saved one. The next ball Ibrahim played to cover and scampered off for a single. Shute Banerjee fielded the ball and could have effected Balooch's run out, but didn't. The year was 1944 and Ibrahim had carried his bat for 137. This was the same game in which an injured Mushtaq Ali (captain of the Muslims) went out to bat with three wickets down against the doctor's instructions. Mushtaq Ali, ever the romantic, scored 36 and after his departure Ibrahim and Amir Elahi took the Muslims to the doorstep of victory before the mini collapse brought in Balooch. The game was a wonderful advertisement for cricket. Indian cricket was alive and well at the Brabourne Stadium. Among those present in the pavilion were Denis Compton, Douglas Jardine and Wally Hammond. And all of them applauded Ibrahim, who was practically besieged by the crowd.

Not only did the Pentangular walk away into the sunset; the hold of the princes who had dominated Indian cricket concurrently began to diminish with the onset of independence. With just privy purses for financial support, they could not finance teams or hire players of repute any more. The era of the professional which had been jumpstarted with Amar Singh, Vinoo Mankad and Lala Amarnath, all of whom played in the Lancashire league was taken to the next level when Vijay Manjrekar and Subhash Gupte followed them to England and then played for several states in domestic cricket. Significantly, Lala Amarnath, a farmer's son who worked in the Railways led this 'masses replacing the classes' theory in Indian cricket. Humiliated on the 1936 tour of England by the Princes, namely Maharajkumar of Vizianagram, Amarnath, one of the most doughty individuals Indian cricket has seen, was now riding shotgun. As somebody wrote, "The hold of the Princes symbolically was over even as India became independent." Amarnath was leading India to Australia on the first post-War tour. The umbilical cord had been cut with the past where Princes had held sway. Richard Cashman writing in *Golden Age of Indian Cricket*, says that: "Princes were forced to prune their cricketing ventures, to dismantle their teams and terminate cricketing appointments." The paradigm had changed in free India and cricket in many ways was beginning to make inroads into the consciousness of the middle class. Business houses and banking establishments were the recruiters in the new age. Cricket on communal lines was giving way to the genesis of the age of commercialism in cricket. The swinging nineties were still a long way off, but the seeds had been planted in the 1950s when the wannabe states wanting to prise open the seemingly impregnable Bombay bastion began to lure quality players with monetary inducements.

Like Vinoo Mankad who coached several youngsters in Bombay, Vijay Merchant groomed others. Merchant and Champakbhai Mehta were contemporaries and in the early

1930s, the duo along with L.P. Jai, Soli Colah and Homi Vajifdar were seen as the rising stars in Indian cricket. Merchant boycotted the trial matches in Lahore prior to India's first tour of England because of the civil disobedience movement, which had been launched in Bombay those days. This element of nationalism saw Vijaybhai, Champak Mehta and L.P. Jai boycott the tour of England, since all three played for the Hindus. Always seen as an understudy to L.P. Jai, Vijaybhai was perhaps the most knowledgeable and technically correct of Indian batsmen. Raiji and his brother Madan also played a lot of cricket in that era. Raiji says, "Vijaybhai was a personal friend and I played under him in 1941. Playing for CCI, we once had a partnership of 187 against Parsi Gymkhana with both of us scoring centuries." Comparing the two Vijays, Raiji says that Hazare had more strokes, though his stance was a little ungainly, while Merchant had more polish and finesse in his batting. He says, "I think both of them were equally good. And let me add that Sunil Gavaskar was in the same league." Hazare who was ADC to the Maharaja of Baroda played the Pentangular regularly between 1937 and 1944 and his rivalry with Merchant is part of Bombay's cricketing folklore. Raiji says that if he were to accord 95 marks to Merchant, then as the examiner, he would give 93 to Hazare. Both were class acts and have the record to prove it. If Merchant excelled in England, then Hazare did so in Australia against Bradman's Invincibles. Amazingly, Merchant and Hazare often reserved their best for the Brabourne Stadium—Merchant notched up 19 centuries (all in first class cricket) with 8 double hundreds and one triple century, while Hazare who was from Baroda and hence played a lot less at the CCI scored 18 hundreds, including three double hundreds and one triple century.

The Pentangular had seen many impressive performances; P. Baloo who took 75 wickets for the Hindus in 15 matches; H.D. Kanga who scored 1015 runs in 24 matches for the Parsis with an unbeaten 233 as his highest; leg spinner S.M. Joshi of the Hindus who took 97 wickets in 22 matches; Prof D.B. Deodhar who scored 1543 runs for the Hindus in 31 matches with 135 as his highest; Homi Vajifdar who scored 1201 runs for the Parsis in 28 matches with 118 not out as his highest; Frank Tarrant of the Europeans who scored 480 runs and took 70 wickets in just 8 matches; L.P. Jai who scored 1284 runs for the Hindus in 25 matches with 156 as his highest; R.J.D. Jamshedji who took 76 wickets in 13 games for the Parsis; Syed Wazir Ali who scored 1268 runs in 19 matches for the Muslims with 197 as his highest; C.S. Nayudu who took 92 wickets in 13 games for the Hindus; Amir Elahi who took 105 wickets for the Muslims in 16 matches among others. Those who stood taller than all these with performances which bordered on the sublime were C.K. Nayudu who scored 2156 runs with 155 as his highest in 30 matches and took 38 wickets to boot; Vijay Merchant, also of the Hindus who scored 1965 runs with 250 not out as his highest in a mere 19 matches; Vijay Hazare playing for the Rest scored 1212 runs in just 8 matches with 309 as his highest and Russi Modi of the Parsis who also played 8 matches scoring 715 runs with 215 as his highest.

Brabourne Stadium then saw Bombay's players flower

in the Ranji Trophy. Vijay Merchant scored 359 not out against Maharashtra in 1943-44 when Bombay was precariously poised at 90 for 5. Merchant and Russi Modi (168) added an unfinished 371 runs for the sixth wicket. Ajit Wadekar slammed 323 against Mysore in 1966-67, while Gavaskar scored 282 against Bihar in 1971-72. The Bombay versus Mysore match of 1966-67 vintage is typical of Bombay cricket in that era. In this Ranji semi-final, Mysore batting first scored 350 with skipper V. Subrahmanyam leading the way with 125. Subrahmanyam was delighted because he had Prasanna and Chandrasekhar in his armoury and he thought that with 350 runs behind them, this would be Mysore's defining moment in Ranji history. Alas, it was not to be as the left-handed dasher Ajit Wadekar just blew the two spinners away with his bat. His score 323. Later bested by Sunil Gavaskar 340 vs Bengal and Sanjay Manjrekar 377 against Hyderabad who torpedoed Merchant's record. Such was Bombay's dominance even in the early years of the championships that Merchant and Modi both scored double centuries, 217 and 210 respectively, against Western India in 1944-45, while Dattu Phadkar 217 and G.S. Ramchand 230 not out replicated that feat against Maharashtra in 1950-51. Merchant and Modi added 373 for the third wicket in that game against Western India while Merchant's brother Uday and Vasant Raiji's brother Madan added 360 for the fifth wicket in 1947-48 against Hyderabad.

In another famous exhibition of batsmanship and what old timers describe as one of the greatest Ranji Trophy games, Bombay played Holkar in the final in 1944-45.

Bombay won scoring 462 and 764, while Holkar scored 360 and 492. Vijay Merchant scored 278, while Mushtaq Ali hit two hundreds in the match, 109 and 130, and Russi Modi missed the feat scoring 98 and 151. But the honours went to Denis Compton playing for Holkar who smashed the Bombay bowling remaining unbeaten with 249. For the last wicket Compton and Rawal (11) added 109, with Compton going just berserk.

Merchant, a Gujarati businessman, was scion of the Vithaldas Thackersay mills and a protégé of another Gujarati batsman L.P. Jai, while Hazare, a Maharashtrian Christian, took up employment first with the Maharaja of Dewas. The Maharaja Vikram Singh's brother-in-law, the Raja of Jath imported Australian leg spinner Clarrie Grimmett to teach him how to bowl leg spin. Vikram Singh asked Hazare to help out. Grimmett soon realised that Hazare would not make a leg spinner, but he worked on his patience and judgement. Just as Bert Wensley had coached Vinoo Mankad in the Jamsaheb of Nawanagar's province (he even led them to the Ranji Trophy title in 1936-37), Grimmett played a role in Hazare's development, bowling at him from 12 yards. The awkward stance notwithstanding, Grimmett saw that Hazare was a batsman with potential and the ability to play big innings. In fact, Hazare went on a private tour to England in 1938 where he saw the best of English and Australian batsmen including Bradman and Hammond. Hazare itched to get a crack at international teams. Both Merchant and Hazare in fact, couldn't play enough Test cricket as a result of the War. Similarly, another great from that era, C.K. Nayudu, was in the employment of Maharaja Yeshwant Rao of Holkar. Holkar tried its level best to take on Bombay and with the Nayudu borthers—C.K. and C.S., Mushtaq Ali and his brother Ishtiaq Ali and even that brilliant sportsman Denis Compton in its ranks—was a force to reckon with. Holkar won the Ranji Trophy in 1945-46, 1947-48, 1950-51, 1952-53, all four times with Colonel C.K. Nayudu leading them.

Merchant can best be described by that doyen of English cricket writers John Arlott who wrote, "Merchant's physical quality is neither the massive might nor the whipcord leanness of other great batsmen. There is something softly feline about him—at the wicket, shirt and sweater heavy to wrists, thick white muffler at his throat—but the stroke, for all its control, is flash-fast because ignoring the bowler's hand, he plays every ball strictly off the pitch. His batting technique is never violent, he seems to have an unvarying system of ball valuation which controls his batting reflexes." Like the great Parsi cricketer Col. Keki Mistry who was once likened to Clem Hill, Merchant was synonymous with precision and technique. Everything was measured and systematic about him at the batting crease. Stance, strokes and adroitness are what old timers recall about his batting.

Sunil Gavaskar rekindled memories of the same unhurriedness at the crease and compactness of strokeplay. This tightness in Sunny's game obviously came after long hours of practice at Matunga maidan. The Kanga League and its wet wickets must have helped equally. I never saw Merchant bat, but I did see a lot of Sunil Gavaskar, both in flesh and on the telly, and I am sure there must have been something of Merchant in the Little Master. As my mind's eye switches to rewind, I find Sunil coaxing the ball to the boundary. These are abiding memories of a cricket enthusiast. A famous story about Merchant's amazing ability to score runs in domestic cricket borders on the absurd. It is said that if a bowler beat Merchant in the nets, then the batsman would actually give the bowler the book as a keepsake. Liloo Ashar, a new ball bowler for Siddarth, playing against CCI managed to bowl Merchant at the CCI. So, overwhelmed with emotion was Ashar that he kept shouting—I have bowled him, I have bowled him and ran around the ground, till his teammates had to calm him down. Such was the halo around Merchant's batsmanship.

Merchant first as cricketer and then as administrator was instrumental in Bombay's rise and rise in domestic and international cricket. He was the first icon, well remembered by all those associated with him. Though many believed that he never quite forgot losing the captaincy to Nawab of Pataudi Senior for the 1946 tour of England and as such systematically dismantled the Nawab of Pataudi Junior's regime towards the latter part of the 1960s, the last word should go to Raiji. Raiji says, "Vijaybhai's outlook was that if something were to benefit Indian cricket, then he was all for it. I don't think he was petty minded, he was a thorough gentleman who bore no grouse." He would tell Raiji, "I cannot coach for I can't impart tips about technique, but I can spot talent with temperament and provide the necessary impetus to push him to the top." It is said that Merchant saw his own likeness in young Sunil Gavaskar. Merchant himself was all praise for Gavaskar, saying, "He has the rare ability of making strokes from the very first over, while I was a safety first batsman. Sunil's advantage is that he is prepared to take calculated risks in his batting and thus able to score more often and faster than I did." To recount an apochrypal story, in 1964 a documentary was shot by Zul Vellani—*The Spirit and Technique of Cricket* where several prominent cricketers were asked to show different facets of the game. Vijay Merchant was convinced to show his incomparable late cut. One of the schoolboys asked to field that day was Sunil Gavaskar. Apparently Kailash Gattani was one of the bowlers doing duty that day and he was quite quick those days. To a ball pitched outside the off stump, Merchant executed the late cut with great precision. Among the onlookers were Mansur Ali Khan Pataudi, Farokh Engineer, Ajit Wadekar and a boy called Sunil Gavaskar. Incidentally, Merchant had picked up the bat after almost 10 years that afternoon. When India was readying to tour the West Indies in 1970-71, young Sunil Gavaskar was practising in the pre-tour nets and Raj Singh standing and watching with Merchant is reported to have asked—who is this boy? Merchant's answer, very short and cryptic—"this boy will score a lot of runs"—prophetic words indeed from one master about another.

There are many in Indian cricket that would disagree that Merchant wasn't vindictive. But that is politics and not cricket! And Indian cricket has seen enough backroom politicking and palace coups.

8 | Powerhouse

A DUSKY BOMBAY EVENING AND A LONE BATSMAN practices in the nets at the Cricket Club of India. Seeking perfection, he tries to play straight, middling the ball, following the famous maxim which Ranji had relayed to C.K. Nayudu—*balla seedha rako, jore se maro, ghabrao mat*! The legendary Ranji's equally famous nephew K.S. Duleepsinhji, the champion batsman and superlative strokeplayer from the mystical Orient standing behind the nets says, "Come on boy, hit him, loft him. Come on play your shots, stop dawdling." The lone man practicing is Madhav Apte, later to play for Bombay and India. But let the dapper Apte tell us the rest, "Duleepsinhji was chairman of the UPSC and a regular at the CCI. I would take every opportunity to sit down with him and discuss cricket endlessly. My idea was to listen to him as he held forth on the finer points of batsmanship." Bombay cricket benefited more from this culture of sharing. An exchange of views and an interface that enriched the game's rising stars. Educating them by tapping into their mental quotient, just as tales of what players from the past had done or achieved plugged into the emotional quotient. This heady cocktail was a booster, the inter-mingling of legendary names with youngsters keen to find their feet, an elixir for the game's growth.

If Vinoobhai and Vijaybhai, as they are affectionately called in Mumbai, touched the lives and careers of innumerable up and coming players, then there are those whose careers were shaped by them. In course of this treatise, I have mentioned Eknath Solkar as one who was tutored and promoted by both. Vinoobhai's own son Ashok was taught by the father and given his big break in international cricket by Merchant as chairman of the selection committee in 1969. Madhav Apte was another who was closely associated with both at one time or the other. If luck starts at your birth, as the saying went in Bombay cricket during those pristine days, then Apte had all the right credentials as he began to move up the ladder. But, sheer determination and hard work were very much part of his make up as well. Apte used to practice in front of the mirror just as young Sanjay Manjrekar did many years later when on the verge of his first hundred against the West Indies at Barbados. A cricket junkie, Apte, now 69, still plays Kanga League for Jolly CC in his familiar Harlequin cap. Apte, who began his Test career excellently, got a raw deal from the selectors, but continued playing, captaining Bombay to Ranji titles twice. Apte played club cricket in Australia as well in the sixties just to get a feel of what the game Down Under was like.

Tracing the genesis of Bombay's batting czars, Apte says, "A child enjoys the game and decides to pursue it further. Maharashtrians by and large aren't a business community. For a lot of them cricket became a means to get a job and consequently gain an element of stability. Cricket became an anchor." Apte, who played for 15 years, was part of a nucleus of the Ranji Trophy-winning Bombay side, a cricketer who retired almost simultaneously—alongwith Manohar Hardikar, Ramakant Desai and Baloo Gupte. When Apte broke into the Bombay side, he was a little over 19 and the team had names like Merchant, Modi, Mankad, Mantri and Phadkar playing.

Apte had scored close to 3000 runs that season in different grades of cricket. He was hoping for a place in the Bombay all-star 14 on the strength of those performances. Apte, a former president of the CCI says, "My disappointment was that I wasn't in the 14." Providence smiled. As luck would have it, Vijay Merchant dropped out of the first game versus Saurashtra from a knee injury, and did not play that entire season. Apte drafted in at the last moment played and scored a hundred. Apte had arrived by taking the place of his mentor Vijaybhai in the Bombay side. Apte says, "Vijaybhai had known me as a child. In our Peddar Road house in Mumbai, the ground floor tenants were related to Vijaybhai. So, he was a regular at the house to play tennis." Apte himself, like several other players of the past, was a good all-round sportsman (Madhu Patil was a good doubles badminton player, as was Bapu Nadkarni;

Polly Umrigar played good table tennis while Sunil Gavaskar still plays a game of badminton at the Bombay Gymkhana whenever he is in India). Apte's favourite was tennis and he won the doubles at Hindu Gymkhana where Vijaybhai was the chief guest. In school cricket, Apte bowled leg spin and once spun out the opposition in the Giles Shield, taking all 10 wickets (1944).

Apte joined Elphinstone College on finishing school. He says, "Dattu Phadkar was to be our coach, but he left for Calcutta and was replaced by Vinoo Mankad." Apte, an Arts student, keen on cricket and always zealous, would be the first to arrive in the morning along with the groundsman for the practice nets. Vinoobhai who used to be hovering around asked young Apte to bowl at him. Apte recollects that he bowled a googly that bowled Vinoobhai through the gate. Impressed, he asked Apte his name. When Apte replied Madhav Apte, Vinoobhai immediately connected, saying—are you Bhau Apte's son? With a relationship established, Vinoobhai began to work on Apte's game. Apte who used to bat at number 10 was asked to open the batting. And as Apte says, "As luck would have it, this worked very well, for Elphinstone had very good new ball bowlers. A new ball used to cost three rupees those days and the college had an annual cricket budget of Rs 1500, so there were new balls aplenty. This sharpened my reflexes and game."

And guess what? Madhav Apte made his Test debut against Pakistan in 1952-53 at the CCI (3rd Test). Alongside him was Vinoo Mankad. The wheel had come full circle. The man who turned him into an opener was batting alongside him. Apte and Mankad had two partnerships in the match, 55 in the first innings and an unfinished 45 in the second as India won the game by 10 wickets. Apte thinks that Vinoobhai played a paternal role in his cricket development. When Apte was picked to tour the West Indies in 1952-53, Vinoobhai and he were cabin mates on the ship, roommates throughout the tour and batting mates on the ground. In the third Test at Port of Spain, when Apte got 163, Vinoo Mankad got 96 run out, batting at number eight. Together they put on over 150 runs.

Merchant who had once asked young Apte at the prize giving ceremony at Hindu Gymkhana whether he would concentrate on cricket or tennis would have been very happy to see Apte as a stable opener for India. But that was the era when players were discarded without so much as a by your leave. Apte whose scores in Test cricket were 30, 10 not out, 42, 64, 52, 64, 9, 0, 163 not out, 15, 33 never played for India again. What does Apte have to say about the vagaries of selection? He says, "Prima facie, it would appear to be selectorial whims, but maybe it's my family background since I came from a wealthy business family. Maybe I rubbed somebody the wrong way, but I always believed that I would return to the Test side. In 1959, my brother Arvind went to England, but I couldn't ever make a comeback." Incidentally, the Apte brothers became one of six pairs to play Test cricket for India.

Ashok Mankad in an earlier chapter spoke about his father Vinoobhai's eagle eye. Vinoobhai, many like Raj Singh Dungarpur believe, was the only real cricketer-coach this country has produced. If he could spot Apte's batting talent, then he could similarly mould Bapu Nadkarni's bowling. One of India's most durable all rounders, Nadkarni was also touched by Mankad. Nadkarni, soft spoken and erudite was part of a spin trinity which served Indian cricket well. Just prior to the dominance of the quartet, it was Nadkarni, Salim Durrani and Chandu Borde who were calling the shots. Nadkarni's idol was Vinoo Mankad. But Nadkarni was a medium pace bowler who played inter-varsity cricket. When Nadkarni came to Pune from Nasik, it was Mankad who spotted him; taking him aside and encouraging him to bowl like left arm spin. Mankad saw that Nadkarni, though slow medium pace, concentrated on line and length. By 1955-56 against the visiting New Zealanders, Mankad was leading the West Zone team with Nadkarni and Chandu Borde in it. Underbowling himself, Mankad allowed Borde (five wickets) and Nadkarni (three) to win the match. Nadkarni says, "He was the master of flight and though I was flatter, I was accurate. Mankad encouraged me to focus on length."

Nadkarni came to Bombay subsequently and played in a crack championship-winning outfit. Discipline and winning seemed to go hand in hand with Bombay cricket those days. Apte says, "Right through one's career, self-discipline remained the buzzword with all of us." While captaining Elphinstone in the inter-collegiate final against Siddarth, Madhav Mantri was the coach. Elphinstone chasing 180 odd to win were 120 for two, comfortably placed, with Madhav Apte batting at 70. Apte was given out caught behind off Surendra Rege in what appeared to be a doubtful decision. On being given out, Apte tapped the ground with his bat and walked off the playing area. Mantri, ever vigilant and upholder of the gentleman's game's values was waiting in the tent. Looking at Apte, he said—I am ashamed of you, the umpire's decision is final, why did you show your reluctance to leave?

Apte was never captain of Bombay for a full season, but he led the side to victory in the Ranji Trophy when players like Umrigar were away. In fact, Apte was dropped from the side and approached by Cricket Association of Bengal vice-president Amar Ghosh, and he played for the Eastern state. Apte, always a Bombay cricket groupie, believes that while Vijaybhai and he shared a textile mill owner background, cricket was the best leveller for it teaches one that there is nothing to be taken for granted and more importantly there is no replay. During the 15-year championship-winning streak, Bombay was a powerful juggernaut, which could do no wrong. As Nadkarni says, "Yes our batsmen were run hungry, but one must remember that we had one of the best spin attacks in the domestic game—Baloo Gupte, Sharad Diwadkar, Manohar 'Manya' Hardikar and myself. We could get any side out for 275 or thereabouts. We had that jagged edge when it came to delivering the knock out punch."

Winning the Ranji Trophy remained a pipedream for Rajasthan in that era, even as it had many 'star' imported players. Rajasthan lost the 1960-61, 1961-62, 1962-63, 1963-64, 1965-66, 1966-67 and 1972-73 finals. Raj Singh Dungarpur played all of them and led Rajasthan in three of those finals. He says, "The Bombay team of the 1960s could have easily defeated the present Indian team,

Tendulkar included." Strong words from one known never to mince words. Sitting in the CCI foyer, Dungarpur says that he knows from personal experience, as he played in all those matches. Reminiscing about the old days, Dungarpur says that the Bombay-Holkar final of 1951-52 played at the CCI was simply of the highest quality, "Everyone that played in that game was outstanding." The game Dungarpur is referring to is the one in which C.K. Nayudu; all of 56 years old was struck on the mouth by Dattu Phadkar's bouncer. Nayudu spat the teeth out, swept them off the pitch and took fresh guard. Dungarpur says, "Bombay was cricket's El Dorado. The best players were participating in the Times Shield—even Durrani, Hanumant Singh, Pataudi and Abbas Ali Baig would come and play in Bombay. There was charm; glamour and the competitive edge which saw quality cricket being played. Let me give you my own example, I was a Ranji player who came to Bombay. But I couldn't make the CCI side those days, and now we are struggling to field an XI. Take the case of Hoshi Amroliwala, who was such a fine batsman, but he couldn't play for Bombay."

After independence, Rajasthan, which was formed by merging various Rajput principalities, became a cricket power, following in Baroda's footsteps. If the Gaekwads were instrumental in Baroda's rise, then Bhagwatsinghji of Mewar was at the forefront of making Rajasthan a powerful cricketing entity. Ramachandra Guha writing in *Wickets in the East* traces the evolution, "Bhagwatsinghji opened the batting for Rajasthan and on the Mewar staff were cricketers like B.B. Nimbalkar, leg spinner C.G. Joshi and that prince charming amongst commoners, Salim Durrani." Bhagwatsinghji was obsessed with winning the Ranji Trophy and he took a vow that if Rajasthan ever won the Ranji Trophy, he would take a dip in the Holy Ganges. Vinoobhai, Manjrekar, Subhash Gupte, G.S. Ramchand, among others were lured by lucre which in any case is the best lubricant, to play for Rajasthan. Salim Durrani was a wicket keeper; he actually played for Central Zone in that avatar against the West Indies in 1958-59. Durrani, a maverick, was also taught the art of left arm slow bowling by Vinoo Mankad and actually won India many matches with his armer.

Ultimately it took the considerable talents of Gundappa Vishwanath, Brijesh Patel, Erapalli Prasanna, Chandra and Kirmani to dislodge Bombay. It was *circa* 1974 and Bombay was playing Karnataka in the Ranji Trophy semi final. Vishwanath scored 162 and Patel 112 as the south-siders reached over 400. And Pras bowls Gavaskar to nip ahead in the psychological battle. Wadekar is run out and with Pras chipping away to take 5-117 in 62 overs, the door is shut in Bombay's face after a glorious reign of 15 years. With Karnataka defeating Rajasthan who remained bridesmaids to win the championhships, Bombay smarting come roaring back to win the Ranji Trophy for the next three years. In 1977-78, Karnataka won the championships again, but by then the balance of power was beginning to shift in Indian cricket. Delhi with several Test cricketers and led by Bedi were beginning to make an impact.

A key member of Bombay's spin quartet in the winning sides of the sixties was Sharad Diwadkar. Nadkarni feels that the Bombay team was also blessed with good all rounders. Both Nadkarni and Diwadkar were dependable lower order batsmen, who have pulled the chestnuts out of the fire on more than one occasion. Nadkarni will tell you how Diwadkar slammed 188 against Rajasthan in a Ranji final, while he himself did the same against Delhi in the 1960-61 semi-final, also at the same venue. Diwadkar had done so on a greenish track, while Nadkarni came in at 27 for 3 with swing bowler Rajinder Pal looking dangerous. Bombay's elder statesman Polly Umrigar was batting with young Nadkarni when Rajinder Pal decided to show some typical north Indian aggro. Just as Eknath Solkar had handled Pandurang Salgaonkar with great felicity (Bapu Nadkarni was Bombay's manager in that match), Bapuji took on Pal. Pal began to glare at Nadkarni, bowled a couple of whistling bouncers and the hunt was afoot.

Then Pal threw in a couple of choicest abuses to unsettle young Nadkarni who countered—"*Maro jore maro, dekho agar mein out hota hoon*—bounce *kar, main tere ko marta hoon.*" Telling words those and sounds like good bravado. A perturbed Umrigar came down the wicket and tried to calm Nadkarni down, but to no avail. As Nadkarni told Umrigar—if he keeps bowling bouncers, then we can either avoid them or play our shots, if he bowls up to us, then the ball will swing and we are likely to get out! Nadkarni was a good hooker and that day he simply annihilated the Pal led Delhi bowling attack. It was a brilliant psychological ploy and Nadkarni was triumphant scoring an enterprising unbeaten 280 odd.

Small grounds and good wickets always enabled

batsmen to flower in Bombay. But there have been instances when bowlers have been rewarded in spades. Apte remembers his very first Test against Pakistan at the CCI in 1952-53. He says, "The wicket looked as it would give assistance to the bowlers, as those days the wicket wasn't covered. Lala Amarnath was captain while Vinoobhai was vice captain. Lalaji held a team meeting where Vinoobhai advised him to induct the opposition in. Lalaji asked—what will the press say? But Vinoobhai prevailed and Pakistan batting first were done in by Lalaji (four) and Phadkar (two) who exploited the dew to have Kardar's Pakistan limping at 60 for 6."

Diwadkar, now Board of Control for Cricket in India executive secretary was an off spinner and a lower order bat who many believe was unfortunate not to play for India. After playing for Matunga Gymkhana, Diwadkar played for Bombay when Ramnath Kenny was dropped against Maharashtra. He too broke into a team that had stalwarts from wall to wall in the dressing room. He says, "Polly Kaka, Apte brothers and Russi Modi were the dominant names then." Modi was an exquisite touch player, all silk and wrist. Those days the Ranji Trophy was played on a knock out basis, so Modi used to score 1000 runs in a season regularly. Modi was also a keen student of the game and though he turned largely reclusive after retiring from the game, his ability to impart learning to youngsters is well known in Bombay cricket. Dilip Sardesai used to work and play for ACC, where Russi Modi was his boss. One morning after watching Sardesai the previous evening in the nets, Modi called on the young batsman and told him his flaws.

Modi, always impressed with Sardesai's ability to bat, then put in a word to his best friend Lala Amarnath who was then chairman of the selection committee to watch the boy from Goa. Soon, Sardesai was playing for India.

These strong links have guided the destiny of Bombay's cricket. If Sachin today says that he wants to spend time with Vinayak Mane and talk to him about the finer points, then the same cycle is extending itself. Diwadkar played for the first time in 1957-58, when Bombay were beaten in the league and Baroda with Vijay Hazare, Kishenchand, D.K. Gaekwad and Mamasaheb Ghorpade won the title. Diwadkar like many other Bombay players can never forget the kinship that existed amongst the players. He says, "From the time we used to leave Bombay Central station, we would be together, playing rummy at one paisa a point. The team would eat together and after a game gather in the captain (Polly Kaka's) room, sing and share stories. The younger lot would listen attentively. Farokh Engineer and Sudhakar Adhikari were the life and soul of these trips." After the match and a shower, the players would devour tea trolleys laden with keema samosas and mixed bhajiya. The players those days used to get Rs 15 per match as allowance and yet they played to enjoy and win.

Diwadkar remembers how he bowled to all three Vijays—Merchant, 'Rao' Hazare and Manjrekar in local cricket. There were battles within battles—games within games as the spirit of cricket was sacrosanct. Diwadkar concedes that he did get two of the Vijays, but never managed to get Merchant's wicket. The crowd-pulling ability of the three Vijays was a foregone conclusion in

Bombay cricket. Crowds used to flock to grounds when Merchant would play for Fort Vijay, or Hazare would turn out for Catholic Gym in Police Shield or Manjrekar would play for SPG. If SPG-DU battles had their own flavour, then the batting of the three Vijays had an ethereal quality attached to it, according to Diwadkar. Raj Singh says that Alec Bedser, that pasha of seam bowling, once told him that barring Bradman, Merchant was the best overseas batsman he had bowled too. Diwadkar bemoans the fact that one-day cricket is killing quality spin bowling. He says, "Spinners have forgotten how to flight the ball. The combat between a batsman who uses his feet and a bowler who flights the ball is completely absent today."

If an ailing Duleepsinhji watched and offered tips to youngsters in Bombay, it was because players of his reputation and calibre were looking to see growth and stimulus. Madhav Apte once asked Duleep—"Sir, why don't you write your autobiography and recount stories of Jardine and your uncle Ranji?" Duleep, ever the prince and gentleman said—"Maybe... someday, I will write it. If I do, I know what I will call it: *If the English Summer Never Comes Again*." Essayist E.V. Lucas in a celebrated piece had written, "I couldn't care if an English Summer never comes again, for Duleep will not be able to play cricket again." Duleepsinhji couldn't tour Australia in 1932 because one of his lungs was damaged and he had to recuperate in a Swiss sanatorium. For as A. Thomson wrote, it was a hard row to hoe for Duleep as he walked in his uncle Ranji's footsteps. Raiji says that Kumar Shri Duleepsinhji continued to work for the betterment of cricket even after this illness prevented him from playing. A regular at the CCI, Duleep would talk to cricketers endlessly about the theory and practicalities of the game. It was always cricket and not his own exploits, which he reminisced about. Duleep never played for India, but those who have followed him and some of the outstanding batsman from Bombay, have chiselled his memory with deft and fine strokes.

9 The Outsiders

BOMBAY WAS CENTRAL, WROTE SALMAN RUSHDIE, SINCE all rivers flowed into its human sea. Emerging out of the mass of humanity are tough cookies, hardened and conditioned by the environment. If Bombay is driven by its own energy source, then the people who inhabit it are plugged into part of a strange testosterone-led high. Ravi Shastri is genetically a non-Mumbaikar, but in every regard he typifies the vitality, vigour and character of the melting pot. Tough, unyielding and even a touch arrogant. But as he says, what the hell, that is the only way to play the game. Influenced at a young age by the image of Ian Chappell, Shastri felt this was the only way to personal nirvana. Shastri says, "From a young age, I became ruthlessly competitive. My motto was that once I crossed the boundary line, there is no senior or junior on the playing field." Following the maxim—If you can't stand the heat, stay out of the kitchen—to the hilt.

That doesn't sound like what was once taught on the playing fields of Eton, but cricket has evolved into war, turning into a metaphor for nationalistic aspirations. Shastri's approach was to go for the jugular, whether bowling or batting. Having scored 3830 runs in 80 Tests with 11 hundreds and 151 wickets to boot, Shastri emerged as one of the top spin bowling all rounders in Indian cricket. From a young age, Shastri developed this habit of winning. Schooled in the art of warfare in Giles Shield where his school Don Bosco won the title, Shastri realised that cricket was not only his vocation, but also his metier. Joining Podar College, Shastri now says, "The Giles Shield victory really pumped me up. I would probably have been languishing as a nondescript doctor somewhere. My father, a doctor, realised that I could make it in cricket, so he gave me a couple of years to establish myself." Shastri who was studying commerce was fortunate in that he was called up for Indian duty very quickly. As he began to take the first steps towards greatness, Shastri's interaction with players of yesteryears like Polly Kaka, Dilip Sardesai, Madhav Mantri, Ramakant Desai and Naren Tamhane enabled him to add value to his cricketing knowledge bank.

When he broke into the Bombay team which was a veritable Test XI with Gavaskar, Vengsarkar, Sandeep Patil, Karsan Ghavri, Paddy Shivalkar, Ashok and Rahul Mankad, Eknath Solkar, Shastri learnt the ropes quickly. And then came his entry into the Test team, straight out of Grimm's Fairy Tales, as he was summoned by Sunil

Gavaskar, pulled out of a Ranji game in Kanpur to fly half way around the world to New Zealand. Replacing an injured Dilip Doshi, Shastri took 15 wickets in the series against New Zealand. This was also the time that Sunil Gavaskar was bestriding the Indian cricket firmament like a colossus. The Bombay lobby bogey had resurfaced in a big way and the north wasn't particularly pleased with the way things were progressing. It must be said that Sunil Gavaskar was always at the forefront of protecting the players' interests. Around the same time, the northern lobby was slowly flexing its muscles. Delhi won the Ranji Trophy in 1978-79 defeating Karnataka and followed that up with an even sweeter victory against Bombay in 1979-80. In fact, the Ranji Trophy from being a single horse race, had now become most competitive with Karnataka, Delhi and Bombay fighting for honours.

The resentment against Bombay was growing. Sunil Gavaskar says, "You have to understand the historical perspective. Bombay had been winning the Ranji Trophy and it was the team to beat. Moreover in both the Indian and West Zone teams, the representation of the Bombay players was always on the higher side. The attitude on the other side was, we must show these Bombay chaps their place." Gavaskar also feels that due to this powerful player presence, Bombay officials also began to dominate the board's politics and this didn't go down well with a lot of people. However, he adds that on tour, he found the Bombay boys always most open and willing to mingle with everybody. He says, "I guess this came from our cultural background. Bombay is an open city that welcomes all. This cosmopolitan culture rubbed off on us."

In the 1979-80 loss to Delhi, Shastri saw this change in Indian cricket manifesting itself. Delhi had overcome the big daddies of Indian cricket and they were now bristling with self-confidence. Players from Punjab who had begun to make Delhi their home made the difference in this rise. Bishen Singh Bedi sowed the seeds of this dynamism and his protégé Madan Lal, along with the Amarnath brothers—Mohinder and Surinder, Kirti Azad, Maharashtra import Chetan Chauhan, Sunil Valson, Arun Lal and later Maninder Singh, Raman Lamba and Manoj Prabhakar took this culture to its logical culmination. Delhi-Bombay battles became the talk of domestic cricket just as Mysore-Bombay had been in the past.

Shastri had Paddy Shivalkar to contend with in the Bombay side and yet he managed to surmount all the imponderables and hindrances in his path. He says, "Sunny had tremendous faith in me. The fear of failure did not exist in me. I went to a school called Bombay cricket and the seeds are sown early in life, you never take a backward step, your mindset doesn't entertain failure." Shastri, who batted at number 10 in his first two Tests, moved up the ranks quickly. He entered Test cricket as a left arm slow bowler, the last of the great ones from Bombay, but quickly adapted to opening the innings. On his return to India, in a close opening Test against England at Bombay, Shastri batting at number six in India's second innings scored 33. Gavaskar plumped for the boy. By the time India visited England in 1982; Ravi Shastri was opening with Sunil Gavaskar.

Then came the defining moment in Shastri's career. On the ill-fated tour of Pakistan in 1982-83, Shastri was injured, his webbing had stitches and he had missed four Tests. Shastri, in his seafacing flat in Mumbai's upmarket Worli district says, "Sandeep and I were sharing a room. The tour had been a disaster for us. I hadn't played for a month. Sunil walked in one morning at Karachi and said I was playing and opening the batting. That day and the innings that I played changed my life completely." Imran, Sarfaraz and Tahir Naqqash were handled with aplomb. The bat was right behind the ball and as Shastri says, "Actually, I played a five man Pakistan pace attack—Imran, Sarfaraz, Naqqash, Khizir Hyat and Shakoor Rana (the last two were the umpires). Shastri followed this with another hundred against the West Indies at Antigua. Shastri says that he worked on his batting because he began to enjoy the challenge of facing up to the quicks. He says, "I used to have a special session every morning at 7 a.m against V.S. Patil at Matunga Gymkhana. This practice against 'Marshall' Patil was the best coaching class." Shastri came up from the *maidans*, playing every level of the game with the same gusto and energy levels.

Shastri scored a double hundred in the Comrade Shield and followed it up with two scores of 60 plus and a five wicket haul against Dadar Union in the Purshottam Shield in the run up to a famous Ranji Trophy quarter final in 1993-94 against Karnataka in Bangalore. Bombay was without Vinod Kambli, Sachin Tendulkar and Sanjay Manjrekar who were doing duty for India. Shastri was leading from the front. Karnataka scored 406 and Bombay was looking at taking the first available transport back home, tottering at 174 for six. Shastri and Sairaj Bahutule smashed a 259 run partnership with the former scoring a handsome 150 not out to see Bombay home. This was Shastri's final year in cricket and even at the office level, he fashioned Tatas win in the Times Shield, scoring an unbeaten 250 in the final. Shastri had always played the game with *khunnas*, exemplifying the spirit of no quarter given and none asked for. His big match temperament was second to none. He says, "Mental toughness was inherent, my sole ambition was to perform to the best of my ability against the best attacks. And believe me, this comes from the character of the city that we reside in. One has to compete for everything in Bombay. A cricket team has only 11 players and I knew that I had to break into the XI." Shastri says that there were times initially when he heard whispers that his not being a Maharashtrian would become an impediment. He never let it bother him as he swam with the tide to lead Bombay to the Ranji Trophy in 1993-94 after an eight-year hiatus.

Ravi Shastri was the man who would be king, many saw him being groomed for the top job in Indian cricket by mentor Sunil Gavaskar. But alas, it didn't happen because of his so-called attitude. Shastri always appeared to be a trifle aloof, a touch arrogant, but there is no doubt in my mind that Indian cricket's hunk played the game harder than most. The resolve would often be seen imprinted on his face. Yes, he did lead India to a spectacular win over the West Indies in the Madras Test in 1987-88, but the selectors, despite his having all the necessary leadership qualities never gave him the job. There is a touch of Shastri in Saurav Ganguly, an alert mind, a tough demeanor and a never say die spirit. Shastri's entire persona can be summed up by his own words: I never hid behind petticoats. I played hard and played to win, never worrying about my selection in the team till I retired. My injury in Australia debilitated me, otherwise maybe I could have played on."

When Shastri started out, he bowled in tandem with Dilip Doshi, which meant that India had two left arm spinners, forging a combine. Then it was Maninder Singh and Shastri who bowled together. Towards the latter part of his career, Shastri practically gave up bowling and concentrated only on his batting. From a spin bowler to a bowling all rounder to a batting all rounder, he finally ended as a batsman. Many believe that as a batsman, he displayed courage and grit, not seen since Gavaskar's other opening partner, Anshuman Gaekwad. Vasu Paranjpe says, "Gavaskar taught the Indian team to get behind the line of the ball and meet it with a straight bat. Look at people like Shivlal Yadav, they too learnt the art of standing firm and giving support to the frontline batsmen." Shastri too learnt this when he was thrown into the deep end, but to his credit, he didn't let his captain down. His handling of young Shane Warne on his last tour abroad during his double century is still etched in the memory of cricket cognoscenti. Bill Lawry to this day feels that he hasn't seen better footwork than what Shastri displayed during that innings.

The Mangalore Brahmin missed his date with captaincy after the 1987 World Cup semi-final defeat at the hands of England at the Wankhede stadium. While most of India thought that he would succeed Kapil Dev, the selectors chose another Bombay player, Dilip Vengsarkar, who was senior to the colourful Shastri. If Umrigar, Ramchand and Contractor (who was from Bombay, but played for Gujarat in the Ranji Trophy) had led India in the past, Vijay Merchant ensured that the Indian captaincy came back to the city after almost a decade with the anointment of Ajit Wadekar. When Wadekar was humiliated and hounded out after the infamous 'summer of 42' in England (1974), it was Tiger Pataudi who was brought back against the West Indies. Tiger's famous refrain, all five Tests or nothing saw an engrossing series unfold. In fact, Tiger who as he mentioned to me, was having problems with his eyesight and was only a stopgap arrangement saw Sunil Gavaskar as his logical heir apparent. But Sunny's tryst with greatness was nipped in the bud by Pandurang Salgaonkar. When Tiger pulled out of the second Test at the Kotla, the captaincy sweepstakes saw the usual machinations and internecine sniping. On the eve of the Test match, Delhi's Ram Prakash Mehra announced that Farokh Engineer would be leading the side, but the next morning S Venkataraghavan came out to toss with Clive Lloyd. Bishen Bedi, another contender had already fallen foul of the cricket board.

Tiger played that series only as captain and when India toured New Zealand that winter, Bishen Bedi became captain. Fate intervened here as well, for Bedi couldn't play the first Test at Eden Park and his deputy Gavaskar got the job. Bedi then led India till the tour of Pakistan in 1978. Finally Gavaskar who could have led India much earlier got the hot seat against a second string West Indies in 1979. Bombay had the job once again. Though Gavaskar was labelled a defensive captain, he was a thinking man, straitjacketed perhaps by the fact that he led a weak team and dogged by the expectation syndrome which holds Indian cricketers and captains in the main to ransom. Yet it was Gavaskar who changed the accent in Indian cricket from spin to pace, using the jagged edge of Kapil Dev. With Kapil Dev firing away, Gavaskar plotted the fall of Pakistan's fabled batting in the 1979 series, vanquishing them 2-0. Gavaskar, unlike Wadekar, was an extrovert in that he had an opinion and was willing to voice it. This trait linking up with his constant reproach of the board's attitude towards players' payments made him a force to reckon with in Indian cricket. Moreover, he started writing, voicing his concern about this and that, even as a player. The board always found him a handful. The denizens who manned the board probably saw similar characteristics in Ravi Shastri and hence opted for Dilip Vengsarkar who was more in the Ajit Wadekar mould as far as captaincy was concerned. The Gavaskar-Kapil Dev running battle saw the Indian captaincy being tossed to and fro.

Shastri could have been adventurous, nay even a progressive captain. Gavaskar showed flair when he led India to the World Championships of cricket in Australia, using leg spinner Laxman Sivaramakrishnan as an attacking bowler and Krish Srikkanth as an attacking batsman hitting over the in field. There was also the small matter of a Test victory at Melbourne against a full strength Australian team in 1981. Sadly Gavaskar would fall into a

defensive frame of mind. Most notably against Keith
Fletcher's English side immediately after that thrilling win
over Australia. There was a state of ennui, with Dilip Doshi
bowling six-minute overs. Similarly against England again
in 1984-85, the spectator's agony was compounded with
slow overrates and even slower batting. Both Vengsarkar
and Shastri subsequently annoyed the cricket board's
satraps by taking up cudgels on behalf of the players' action
group, which culminated in a Supreme Court verdict
favouring the players under the MRTP Act. It was then that
a more pliable Srikkanth and Mohd. Azharuddin took over
the mantle of captaincy. Over the last 30 years, Wadekar,
Gavaskar, Vengsarkar and Tendulkar have had longish
stints as captains of India. Strangely, Azharuddin has had
the longest. Tendulkar too, unfortunately has fallen into the
Wadekar-Vengsarkar school of captaincy trap. Introverted
Maharashtrian who doesn't like seeking counsel and
communicates poorly with the world at large. Gavaskar
was a good communicator, while Shastri, flamboyant and
an extrovert had public relations problems. Tendulkar has
had two stints as captain of India and there is no doubt that
he will get another shot, but before that he has to open up.
This transition is beginning to take shape in the new Sachin,
as has been detailed in an earlier chapter.

Long before Ravi Shastri arrived in Bombay and Indian
cricket, there was another outsider who carved a special
niche for himself in the annals of the city's cricketing
history. Gulabrai Ramchand was also an all rounder, and he
opened the bowling for India for many years. Ramchand
blended well with the cricketing background of Bombay.

Ramchand says, "I moved out of Karachi in 1946 when Jasu Patel who was from Ahmedabad asked me to come to the city on the banks of the Sabarmati." Ramchand stayed with Patel's family and completed his graduation there. He never played for Gujarat though for when the Ahmedabad based club Baronet CC toured Bombay, Vijay Merchant saw him. Vijaybhai told him—Bombay is the home of cricket and if you are a cricketer then your future is here. Ramchand says, "Vijaybhai encouraged me greatly and helped me get the CCI membership for one thousand rupees. My brother Nanik G.S. was living in Bombay and playing for the Scindias (Allan Sippy who later played for Bombay is Nanik's son)." After missing the 1947-48 Ranji season, Ramchand was playing for Bombay the next year. With K.C. Ibrahim as captain and Polly Umrigar, Russi Cooper, Russi Modi, Madhav Mantri and Dattu Phadkar in the team, Ramchand batted at number nine in his first match.

This is a recurring theme; some of India's better batsmen began their careers batting lower down for Bombay, such was the batting depth. If Shastri with a tyro like Bahutule could win a Ranji quarterfinal without his top three batsmen, it only throws into stark relief the depth and fighting qualities of Bombay cricket. Ramchand says that one would have to perform constantly in local cricket to stay in the Bombay side. Ramchand feels that he was never treated like an outsider, for he learnt Marathi quickly and flourished in Bombay's cricket culture. Ramchand played for Sind, Bombay, for 13 years and finally went to Rajasthan as a professional. Ramchand says that Bombay was a veritable powerhouse with as many as eight players travelling to England in the 1952-tour party. He says, "Ramesh Divecha played for India against England, but couldn't play for Bombay. I very honestly feel that we could have fielded a parallel XI those days which would have thrashed the Rest of India." Ramchand like many Bombay players has a story or two to tell. His favourite story is of Bombay playing in Atul where Polly Umrigar, the captain had to leave midway to attend a national selection committee meeting. The next afternoon Polly was scheduled to return from Bombay. Bombay led by Ramchand (six wickets) and Tiny Desai (four) finished the game in next to no time and met an exasperated Polly Umrigar at the railway station. Polly Kaka too shocked to see his teammates at the station thought the worst, but was stunned when he heard that Bombay had won outright. Bombay's strength, according to Ramchand was that the captain had many bowling and batting options at his disposal.

Depth working in conjunction with resolve: Paddy Shivalkar and Eknath Solkar will tell you of the 1972-73 Ranji Trophy final in Madras. On a Bunsen, Tamil Nadu thought they had Bombay on the mat. Spin twins Vaman Kumar and Venkat wreaked havoc as Bombay were sent into a complete tailspin, bowled out for 160. Tamil Nadu closed out the first day at 60 for 2 and though the celebrations appeared premature, Bombay's epitaph seemed to have been written finally. Paddy and Ekky, bowling left arm spin, something that Vinoobhai always wanted him to bowl just breezed through the TN batting the next morning. The match was over in two and a half days with Bombay winning comfortably. This is the same match in which TN bowler got a hat trick in the Bombay second innings, but all to no avail, for Shivalkar was waiting to bushwhack them all over again in the final essay.

Mihir Bose while describing Ramchand in *History of Indian Cricket* says, "Ramchand brought to the game some of the combative, hustling, business skills which his community was known for. He was a useful medium pace swing and seam bowler, and a hard-hitting lower order batsman who was never afraid to strike the ball." Ramchand in his playing days was an advocate of players' rights. Always quick to get equal rights as visiting sides, Ramchand often fell foul of the board. Ramchand is best remembered for leading the Indian side to victory against Richie Benaud's Australians in 1959-60. Ramchand says, "We were playing on turf for the first time in Kanpur. The choice was between A.G. Kripal Singh and Jasu Patel who had a freakish action. The pitch was softish and Lala Amarnath, chairman of the selection committee plumped for Patel. The result was that Patel took 14 wickets and India won. But it was a team performance." Once when Ramchand had an altercation with a Bombay selector and was dropped, his response on his return to the side after Ramakant Desai was injured was 8-12 against Saurashtra in 1959-60. Even today, Ramchand's exploits in the Ranji Trophy are remembered. He scored three hundreds in three different Ranji semi-finals and four hundreds in four different Ranji finals.

Both Ramchand and Shastri were in many ways

identical—outsiders who made a mark for Bombay and India by merging with the city's cricketing culture. Shastri was born in Bombay and bred on the mean streets and *maidans*, while Ramchand came from Karachi and made it his home. All rounders, they both played the game hard and to win. Naked aggro was what separated them from others of their ilk. That and the fact that they believed in taking no prisoners.

Epilogue

SUPERMAN FLIES FROM METROPOLIS TO OFFER HIS services to the Indian Test selectors, who are meeting in a secret room in an expensive hotel. They look at him suspiciously.

'Can you bat?' they ask.

'I guarantee that I will hit a six off every ball bowled to me and that I will never get out.'

'Can you bowl?'

'I guarantee to take a wicket with every ball I bowl and to bowl all day if need be.'

'Can you field?'

'I guarantee to stop the other team taking any runs off any ball they hit anywhere in the field.'

The selectors mutter among themselves.

'Ah,' they ask at last, 'but are you from Bombay?'—Mike Marqusee in *War Minus the Shooting*.

Vijay Merchant, Sunil Gavaskar and Sachin Tendulkar are in many ways three faces of the same man, essaying the part of creator, preserver and destroyer. They all went to the same school, trained in the rudiments of the same game and have become iconoclasts, running a relay, which goes back nearly seventy years. The school was Bombay and the game cricket. If Vasant Raiji, one of the grand old men of Indian cricket says that he sees L.P. Jai in Sachin Tendulkar, then it is a tradition being carried on by a younger man. Raiji who has his lunch at CCI every working day was watching a young boy blast away in a match. He told his brother Madan, also a cricketer, "I say, doesn't this boy bat like Jai?" And Madan concurred. L P Jai captained Bombay to their first Ranji Trophy victory in the inaugural year of the championships in 1934-35. This was an era where the Ranji Trophy meant nothing as the Quadrangular and Pentangular was the cynosure of all eyes. This was the era of communal cricket and a time when a Parsi didn't want to be captained by a Hindu (Jai). While things have changed in free India, Bombay or Mumbai has lost its pre-eminence. Today Tendulkar ploughs a lone furrow for Mumbai. More often than not, he is the only representative from the city in the Indian side. Ajit Agarkar and Sameer Dighe have been in and out of the side. This is a far cry from the halcyon days when Bombay had a minimum of five players in the national side. The Superman joke mentioned above is a distant reality and a thing of the past.

It isn't that the standard of Mumbai's cricket has deteriorated alarmingly. Think of the rapid strides the game has made elsewhere in the land. With starships beaming images of cricket from faraway places into the living rooms, the message of cricket has spread far and wide. Karnataka and Delhi were the first challengers to Bombay's unparalleled successes. Right through the 1970s and 1980s, they were snapping at Bombay's heels, Karnataka won thrice while Delhi triumphed five times. In those 20 years, Bombay won the title nine times, while in the sixties they had won it all ten times. Hyderabad, once a cricketing power actually won the title in 1986-87 defeating Delhi, while Tamil Nadu managed to do the same the following year. Haryana got its name inscribed under Kapil Dev in that famous final at the Wankhede stadium, while Punjab too managed to win in 1992-93. It is Karnataka, which over the last five years has emerged as the side to beat. With Bangalore having turned into a thriving cricketing centre and Test players coming through an assembly line, this paradigm shift in the nation's cricketing balance had to happen. Karnataka has won thrice in 1995-96, 1997-98 and 1998-99, while Baroda has won the Trophy for the first time since 1957-58 in 2000-2001 thanks to Zaheer Khan. The gospel of cricket has been drummed around the country; players like Debashish Mohanty and Shiv Sunder Das from Orissa, Harbhajan Singh and Yuvraj Singh from Punjab and Zaheer Khan from Baroda have made a name for themselves. Anil Kumble, Javagal Srinath, Rahul Dravid and Venkatesh Prasad have proved to be catalytic agents for the game's mushrooming in Karnataka and Bangalore in particular.

I have written about role models and inspirational factors. Well, the same thing has happened in other parts of India. Ravi Shastri feels that cricket in Mumbai has gone off the boil as Karnataka has become *primus inter pares*. Milind Rege thinks that local cricket doesn't have that edge any more. Top class cricketers have too many international commitments and their absence is eroding the culture that had been built up. If the boys in Chikalwadi used to play matches amongst themselves with a wet tennis ball so that it would sting the adversary, then that 'khunnas' and killer application while still there at a subterranean level is not being able to make an impact. Naren Tamhane thinks that to be fair to Bombay cricket, the others have come on by leaps and bounds. But has Mumbai cricket become complacent? Tamhane says, "What is the association doing? Today Mumbai doesn't have a wicket keeper after Sameer Dighe. There was a time when Bombay had five wicket-keepers jostling for a place in the Bombay side. So much heritage and tradition is not being channelled thoroughly as 300 odd Mumbai clubs are wallowing in a morass of mediocrity.

Inter-school and inter-collegiate cricket is in a similar moribund state. Educational institutions like Anjum-e-Islam, Robert Money, Bharda, Maratha, Bai Kabibai, Balmohan Vidyamandir, Shardashram, King George, Ruia, Podar, Siddarth and Elphinstone among others were the talent wells and ponds, which used to throw up the next generation of stars. Is the malaise serious enough to jeopardise the game's future? Not really. It was triggered off much earlier when Bombay players began to travel to the English leagues and East Africa in search of pelf. Which cannot be held against the cricketers, for they had to earn a living. But when the Kanga League stopped seeing the Test stars in action, the standards came down drastically. However, the age of commerce has led to sweeping changes all over the world. In this environment, old world values seem redundant. Sudhir Naik, who coaches the successful National CC says, "There is too much easy living and very little emphasis on commitment. I notice that the boys aren't fit enough, and very weak in their legs. I remember H.S. Anand, a left arm fast bowler who just knew how to bowl quick. He took over a 100 wickets in the Kanga League and was a terror. Well, he was a natural and with him as our secret weapon we cleaned up the Police and Mahindra Shield." Ramchand adds that crass commercialism has changed the focus and priorities. Bombay's strength, he argues, was its high standard of local cricket. This, he reckons, has gone to seed. Vengsarkar thinks that the focus is not on winning, but on securing a place in the Indian side. Priorities have changed. Vengsarkar says, "This is far removed from the time when we used to play weaker teams in the Ranji Trophy. While we used to practice in the nets, players from the opposition would come and watch. Such was the aura about Bombay and its players."

Ajit Wadekar, captain and manager feels that not only have priorities changed, but so have attitudes. He says, "Everybody wants to become Tendulkar and Kambli. You cannot copy anybody in cricket, talent has to be inherent and hard work is a mantra." He agrees with Vengsarkar saying that the attitude of winning has been lost completely. Wadekar says, "Diwadkar and Ramakant Desai though primarily bowlers in a very strong Bombay batting outfit used to score tons of runs. I think passion and sincerity; two vital ingredients have been lost in this age of commercialisation. I have seen Polly Kaka and Sunny returning from England and play Kanga League." Sunny Gavaskar says that the discipline that a Dadar Union or a Shivaji park taught its cricketers was the best education. He says, "Dadar Union evoked a strange sense of loyalty. Playing for the club meant everything for us. While the intensity of battle was a lot less in the 1970s, the games against Shivaji Park Gymkhana in the Kanga League, Purshottam and Talim Shield were dog fights."

At the same time, there is talk of individualism and how it is taking its toll on Mumbai cricket, even as sides like Punjab, Baroda, Karnataka and UP are playing like cohesive wholes. Old timers remember how Naren Tamhane and Bapu Nadkarni travelled by train to play a Test match. Sudhir Naik is very clear in his mind that today's cricketers are too soft. But Vasu Paranjpe, former national coach and elder statesman of Dadar Union feels that the present generation of players needs to be nursed and nurtured. Most importantly, they need to be given lessons in the history of the game and Mumbai's cricketing tradition. He has high hopes of Vinayak Mane who has all the shots and even scored runs against the visiting Australians. Paranjpe got admission in Elphinstone College only because Madhav Mantri gave him a recommendation letter addressed to the principal N. Ahmed, which simply said—this boy is the best fielder in India. Now, Mumbai cricket languishing under the weight of expectation abounds with memories of a bygone era.

Is Mumbai then a victim of its own hype? No, there was a time when it marched forth like Gulliver in a land of Lilliputians. Cricket in the city was built on a foundation of competition. Now, the rest have caught up as Mumbai's monopoly is diluted. Raj Singh Dungarpur, who has played against Bombay and followed its evolution from a powerhouse into an also ran, says, "Bombay will have to rethink and reformulate its strategy for the future. There are no Tendulkars or Kamblis around the corner. Old heads are applying their minds to alleviate the woes, but I think it is time, somebody from outside is brought in to revamp the game in the city."

An external reality check is what Rajbhai wants. His candidate for Mumbai coach's job is Anshuman Gaekwad. But that won't go down very well with the array of past stars in Mumbai cricket. Yet, he is positive about Mumbai cricket. For his sense of history tells him that Bombay or Mumbai still has it to deliver the goods. Rajbhai says, "I do believe England's flesh was made of south, bones were of north, while the backbone was definitely Yorkshire. Similarly, Mumbai is Indian cricket's backbone. Didn't they defeat Australia at the CCI in 1998?" Yes, but that was a one-man army called Sachin Tendulkar who indulged in a demolition Derby. Rajbhai thinks that even as Yorkshire and Mumbai have slipped down the charts, New South Wales in Australia manages to stay afloat.

Now the Mumbai Cricket Association under the helmsmanship of politician Sharad Pawar has set up a Cricket Improvement Committee. The terms of reference of this committee are for one year. Some of the cricketers whom I met are part of this committee—Madhav Apte, Milind Rege, Lalchand Rajput, Chandrakant Pandit, Raju Kulkarni, Dilip Sardesai and umpire M.V. Gothoskar. Sardesai says, "We are trying to change cricket at the grassroots level. We find that limited overs cricket is impeding the art of building an innings. At the school level itself, we want to usher in longer games. We want to study the faults that have crept into the game at all the levels and then offer our recommendations."

Sunil Gavaskar who heads the board's technical committee and oversees the ICC's technical committee as well adds, "I don't want to be judgemental about Mumbai cricket today. You have to understand that talent has levelled out. The domination and fear that teams had while playing Bombay in the old days has reduced considerably. I remember in our time, if there was a mid-off and an extra cover, the opposing batsman could have walked a run, but such was the fear psychosis that he would think against such an act." In big games, he says, bowlers and batsmen from the other side used to often chicken out. But this Gavaskar argues led to Bombay players having this superior air about them at times. He says, "Bombay players and media would often rubbish players from the other sides. Now it is all even-steven." Gavaskar also feels that once great players emerged from other centres, men like Bedi, Vishy, Pras, Chandra, Brijesh Patel, then the chaps around them started believing in their own ability. And of course began to believe that Bombay was beatable. This sense of compe-tition spurred other sides. Karnataka and Delhi were the pioneers in this regard.

Shastri says that today if you take Sachin Tendulkar out of the Mumbai team, then there is no team left. Which he feels is a great pity. Shastri says, "It is time for the planners and administrators to go beyond the city limits and find talent. Cricket in Mumbai has moved northwards. I think city boys are too soft. We should look at the new talent wells in Bhayander, Kurla, and Kayan-Dombivli. We should look for people who are hungry. Take Sri Lankan cricket, today the best new talent is coming from outside Colombo." Tendulkar moved from Bandra East to train at Shivaji Park. He moved house and school as young boy while his school chum traveled all the way from Kanjur Marg to practice tirelessly under Achrekar's eagle eye. That was the sense of commitment shown by the two youngsters.

Ashok Mankad, another oracle of Mumbai cricket and its most recent coach, however, thinks otherwise. He says, "Let us understand that other teams have improved considerably. Mumbai is still a formidable team; the city has the same cricketing ethos. We don't require committees. Yes, we lost to Punjab, but we don't need to panic. Don't forget, we won nine straight victories last season. I expect Vinayak Mane, Kunal More, Omkar Khanvilkar and Swapnil Hazare to come through as the next wave of players. It is a question of time before the boys start believing that there is a pot of gold waiting for them at the end of the rainbow." Mankad's regret is that young cricketers aren't keeping pace with the change in the game—modern science and bio-mechanics are part and parcel of a more athletic sport.

All in all, it does appear that Mumbai cricket is

struggling to come to terms with the new realities. A surfeit of limited overs cricket at the local level isn't helping matters. The moot point is that the law of averages have caught up with Mumbai cricket. Take the cradle of Mumbai cricket—Shivaji Park—that is often used for political rallies. These are signs of changing times. Great teams like the West Indies and Australia have also seen troughs and peaks, for when a generation of champion cricketers retires, the void is hard to plug, till such time as a new breed surfaces to inherit the mantle. Transition is part of cricketing cycles and right now Mumbai is looking into the barrel of a gun. If Tendulkar can inspire the younger lot of Mumbai's cricketers to greater deeds, then Indian cricket's megastar would have done yeoman service to his city. Bapu Nadkarni thinks that the ills that afflict Mumbai cricket presently are due to an accumulation of over a decade of non-performance. He says, "There are too many diversions for today's youth, I don't see them committing themselves wholeheartedly. This is the difference between the players of today and the past. The hunger is missing." Maybe the edge is missing, maybe the diversions and the art of making money is taking precedence over actually playing the game to the best of their ability. This is a conundrum which players of the past and present are constantly arguing about. Commerce has changed the game unequivocally, and one has to live with that.

Mike Marqusee in his book *War Minus the Shooting* writes, "Delightfully cosmopolitan, chaotically multi-cultural Bombay was being refashioned into straitjacketed Mumbai." Partly true, but cricket is still being played on the mean streets and every Mumbaikar believes it is a matter of time before the next young man with *savoir faire* will come through the kaleidoscope that makes up the city. Economic disparity will propel the young man forward to make his tryst with greatness. It could have been Amol Mazumdar and it might well be Vinayak Mane. It could be Siddarth Manjrekar, Sanjay's son and Vijay's grandson, only a toddler now, but walking in his father and grandfather's footsteps. Let us wait and watch! The Cricket Improvement Committee might not be the cure. Inspirations like Merchant, Gavaskar, Manjrekar and Tendulkar might well do the trick.